Consuming Fire

A Prayer Strategy for Intercessors Enforcing the Kingdom

by

Michael David Riggs

Copyright Page

Published by Access Media, LLC
Huntsville, Alabama

ISBN for Paperback: 978-0-9859593-2-6
ISBN for eBook: 978-0-9859593-3-3

To order copies of this book contact Access Media, LLC at:
P. O. Box 761, Huntsville, AL 35804,
or by email at
michael@accessmedia.co.

Disclaimer

This book is not to be relied upon as any type of formal advice or counseling, but rather as information that has been provided for your guidance, based primarily on the personal beliefs, opinions, and experiences of the author.

The information in this book is provided "as is" for general information only, without any guarantee as to the accuracy or completeness of such information.

The author and publisher are not herein providing any type of advice or service. As such, this information should not be used as a substitute for any type of advice, counseling or consultation.

The author and publisher make no representation, express or implied, with regard to the results of the practice of the methods contained in this book, and accept no responsibility or liability for the consequences of anyone using or relying on this information.

This disclaimer applies to any and all usage of this information, in whole or in part.

References

Most Bible references quoted are from the King James Version (KJV), which is public domain.

Other's will be indicated in the text and with the publisher's requirements.

The Young's Literal Translation (YLT) is used in places and is public domain.

The New King James Version is used and those uses are indicated as required by the publisher as follows: (NKJV™)

Blue Letter Bible online reference source, at www.blueletterbible.org, is used often and uses Genesius's Lexicon for word meanings. Genesius's Lexicon is in the public domain.

Strong's Exhaustive Concordance of the Bible is also used for some of the definitions of words taken from Scripture. These will be indicated.

Bible references not quoted in the text will be included in the Bibliography and indicated in the footnotes.

Acknowledgements

I want to say "thank you" to my Dad and Mom, E. A. and JoAnn Riggs, who taught me the necessity of the Word of God and prayer in my life daily, and who taught me to have a deep love for and trust in God's Word. I am eternally grateful! You have given me my deepest passion and joy in life.

Thank you to my wonderful wife, Denie, who has been my friend and partner, and my comfort, as we have walked through the fire together.

Thanks to Pastor Will Umbarger who, at my request, first prayed for the fire of God to come upon me and surround me as I was, to my knowledge, beginning the process that has become this book.

Thank you to all the many friends who have ministered to me, prayed for me, given me insight and wisdom, done editing, and made so many contributions to this work. Thanks especially for those who invested their time to read this work.

Thank you Julie Mouvery for taking my thoughts and making them reality with the book cover. You did a great job! You always do...

Thank you Rachel Riggs, for your hard work and diligence in editing this book. You are an amazing writer yourself and your insights were excellent.

Thank you Father, Jesus, and Holy Spirit, for Your guidance, teaching, wisdom, protection, provision, Your faithful presence in my life as You continue to lead me along in this work and in life. Thank you for Your amazing fire that is both purifying and protecting - all consuming!

-Michael David Riggs

Preface

As I write this I am facing my 54th birthday in just a couple weeks. I have been committed to serving Jesus and seeing God's Kingdom come on earth as it is in heaven for well over 3 decades. I have also been amazed at how challenging that seems at times, especially when Jesus has given us His power and authority in the earth to fulfill His assignments to us.

I have served as a pastor for 34 years. I was in Christian radio for 14 years where I was shifted into an intercessory position over a population base of nearly one million people. It was there that I first began to understand and experience interceding and speaking prophetically over regions.

I have been involved in marketplace ministry or city reaching efforts for over 20 years now. In any region of the world, this is a sphere of service that God's enemy has had control over for thousands of years. Engaging in this type ministry attracts much warfare.

My wife and I own an international business which is based on Psalm 8:2, in which we teach babies and preschoolers, as well as their parents, to be worship musicians. These silence (or still) God's enemy according to Psalm 8:2. This is a field which causes us to step into extreme war sometimes. The warfare used to be a constant. God has continued to bring us to new levels in Him and in faith.

We have known our share of spiritual warfare, or adversity.

There came a time in my life when I began to come under intense pressure from the enemy, so much so that I wondered what was happening to me. Had it not been for the sweet comfort of the Holy Spirit and God's Word this would have been a very fearful time in my life.

The prayer strategy contained and revealed in this book is one born out of times of deep and intense spiritual warfare. It is a tried and proven strategy that is what God used as my deliverance. This book is not intended to be an exhaustive look at what the Bible has to say about the fire of God, but is simply to share the prayer strategy presented.

I know it has validity for the body of Christ. It has helped me tremendously, and continues to on a daily basis. It is now helping others who are implementing it, and helping their cities...

I know that this book can be a blessing to you in your sphere and region, in your city, in your calling, in your family, and in your life.

I pray that it is...

Michael David Riggs

Foreword

"Michael does an excellent job in communicating how God's consuming fire is to be connected in our family lifestyle. It is the fire of God that extends from His nature but is also to be a part of our lives as we pursue Him. Jesus is that "consuming fire" that dwells within us and is present to transform us into His image by purifying us. It is amazing how this process prepares us for advancement in HIS Kingdom and can release His fire into others. Michael gives insight and a prayer strategy moving us into a position to be a demonstration of His presence by the fire of His presence within us. This will bring personal deliverance, purging, and restoration for every believer to move forward in this new year and ten year season of Ayin. This is a challenging book for every believer to grow and mature in HIM and to take you to the next level."

Chuck Pierce & Linus Vaughn
Glory of Zion International
Global Spheres, Inc.

Table of Contents

Consuming Fire

A Prayer Strategy for Intercessors Enforcing the Kingdom

Introduction

Our God is a consuming fire! We see this presented three times in Scripture verbatim, and many other times in concept.

Why would a God of love express Himself through inspired Scripture as a consuming fire? Why would He draw us to His presence if He is indeed of, or surrounded by, an element that would consume us? *Is it possible that we do not understand the fire of God?*

The reality is that God is in the process of transforming all those who have or will become His people, redeemed by the blood of the Lamb of God, into His likeness—into the likeness of His Son Jesus Christ.

Is it then accurate to say that God's desire is for us, you and me, and all those who are believers in Jesus Christ, to be transformed into consuming fire? I believe it is. God started a process in my life in about 2005 that resulted in my learning a prayer strategy from the Holy Spirit. This is the prayer strategy contained in this book. As I began to think on writing this book I thought I would call it "Our God is a Consuming Fire". I quickly realized that it needed to be called "Consuming Fire", because it is God's purpose to transform <u>us</u> into His fire.

God is a consuming fire. First this is presented in Deuteronomy 4:24. In this context God is dealing with Israel and tells her that if she forgot her covenant with Him and stepped into idolatry He would allow Israel to be scattered, weakened and destroyed among the nations. It's interesting that covenant breaking and idol worship are linked. That's because when we worship anyone or thing other than God we are guilty of breaking covenant, because our covenant is to worship Him. When we break covenant, it is idolatry, and we are subjecting God to a position lower than the one who steals our affection and causes us to break covenant, rather than placing Him as the Most High God, El Elyown. God will be worshipped by His creation, or else that creation will be consumed. This whole thought process is important as related to this book, because God's fire is meant to refine us. Idolatry in each of our lives and bloodlines is at the root of much that the fire of God needs to purge from us. We'll talk about this in concept in this book.

Next, it is in Deuteronomy 9:1-6 that we find God is a consuming fire. In this passage we can see God as the One Who goes before us and consumes the enemy before us. This will be key in our stepping into the fulfillment of Daniel 7 as we pursue possessing and enforcing the Kingdom in days ahead. Key to understanding this is an understanding of the "Anakim" or "Anak". These were giants, "a people great and tall". The word "Anak" actually means "neck" and refers to a people of a long neck, or giants. How interesting..."Anak" equals "a neck"! That's funny. These people were of reputation as an army to be feared according to Deuteronomy 9 which says, "...who can stand against the children of Anak." This is like the picture we have of antichrist in Daniel 7 who will speak great words against the Most High God as he is given the saints into his hand for a season. With a thorough reading of this passage it becomes plain that it will be absolutely necessary for us as the people of God to access the "consuming fire" that is our God to gain victory in this time. This is a very important thing for us to understand, and we will deal with this at great lengths in this book.

The third place that God is presented as a consuming fire is in Hebrews 12:29. This is an incredible passage where we see God presented as a consuming fire in relation to the shaking of the last days when He will establish His Kingdom and bring it into fullness. It is my belief that it will be, it is, the fire of God that causes the shaking of all things. All things are composed of matter and fire has an effect on all matter. It will either consume it or refine it and redefine it. All matter resonates at its own frequency. Fire is frequency and when it is superimposed upon another frequency it changes the state of that frequency, so it changes the state of matter. This is how radio works. An audio sound wave is "modulated" onto a higher or faster wave, called a carrier wave and changes the state of the carrier wave. The changes, or modulations, are what makes for the resulting sound we hear coming out of our radio, to put it very simply. This is how the carrier wave "carries" the sound. When God's fire is released upon structures that have resonated at opposing frequencies they are being altered and they shake. You can actually see this effect in a fire in your fireplace. When you add a new component to the fire the whole fire changes—you can see this change reflected in the color of the fire, the shape and height of the flame, and even in the sound the fire makes. When kingdoms that oppose God's Kingdom and His purpose are touched with the fire of God they begin to change and they begin to shake. All things will be shaken. God will shake all things! This is told to us in Haggai 2 verses 6 and 21, Isaiah 13:13, and then quoted in Hebrews 12:26. This shaking is in the heavens over which God is seated and which contain principalities and powers and the rulers of darkness of the ages. These rulers have had their kingdoms in place for centuries or millennia and as God begins to "modulate" them with His fire they will shake. Modulate is also a musical word. In music it means to change keys, which is to change sound and to change frequency. Believe me, when God begins to impose His fire upon the rulers of the darkness of this world they will be "singing a different tune". They will be seeing their demise and the fact that they must begin to confess Jesus Christ as Lord of all. This is where the word *apocalypse* gets its dark connotation— the apocalypse is nothing more than the revelation of

Jesus Christ and His Kingdom, which will usurp authority over all other kingdoms and rule forever. This is only a bad thing for those kingdoms that oppose the Kingdom of God and His Christ, and those who govern in them. I believe the end time shaking of all things is the apocalypse. God will shake all things, and our God is a consuming fire.

YOU have been chosen by God, your Father, as a vessel of His fire...a carrier of the instrument He will use to consume His enemy little by little. It is time! The day is here!

From 2005 to 2007 I went through a period of mental and spiritual anguish. I sought God about why, about what was going on in me. In about February of 2007 I began to develop a strong desire to have the fire of God come on me in such a way that when I would sense the presence of evil around me, the spirit behind that evil would be consumed by the fire of God surrounding me and in my life. Out of this time _a prayer strategy developed in my life that is the most effective tool of spiritual warfare I've ever experienced in 33 years of pastoring and 18 years of leading regional intercession._

This book has developed out of this desire and resulting prayer strategy.

I want to make it very clear in a book like this that I am writing about spiritual warfare, war against spirits of darkness. This book is about "wrestling against" spirit beings as Paul wrote about in Ephesians 6:12

and II Corinthians 10:3-5. He tells us there that we do not wrestle against flesh and blood. This book is NOT about bringing harm to or wishing harm upon any person, any human being. It is, rather, about spiritual darkness that blinds people being removed so that they can see the truth of Jesus, the Savior and have the opportunity to choose Him, have their relationship with their Creator restored, and thus come into His "life abundant" that He promised us (John 10:10). *Let there be no way anyone draws from this writing any thought or desire to harm any human being!*

We are told of Jesus that He will baptize us with fire. We are told that the fire will try all things and all our work to see of what sort it is and test its eternality. We are urged to come boldly to the throne of grace, God's throne, to have our needs met. Yet that very throne is the mercy seat of the Ark of the Covenant where God's presence falls, the One Who is the consuming fire. We see a river of fire flowing from God's throne that is to consume all His enemies, including the enmity that is in our flesh. In reality this fire simply transforms us into what God is, a being of fire that consumes all that is not like (aligned with) Him. *As we are transformed into His likeness, consuming fire*, we are then enabled to engage the enemy and see him destroyed.

I have to ask you: don't you want relief from spiritual oppression? Don't you want the enemy to have its due? Don't you want payback for the enemy? Aren't you tired of the need for repeat deliverance? Aren't you ready for the time when God will destroy His enemy once and for all, annihilating it?

These are the things that will be dealt with in detail in this book.

"There is coming a day when God will judge His enemies little by little, one by one, and consume them with His fire...I believe we are at that day."

Chapter 1

Fire Invisible to the Human Eye

A couple years ago I was teaching in one of our studios and heating some tea in a paper cup. I was using a microwave that I was not familiar with and set it for 2 minutes. This was a more powerful microwave than I usually use. I left the room and came back to find that after two minutes the paper cup was brown on the bottom, almost in flames, and smoke was coming from the microwave oven. I had almost started a nice little fire!

Microwave ovens have been around for enough decades now that all of us are used to the fact that there is a fire that is invisible to the human eye. It's not hard to convince someone familiar with a microwave oven that there is a heat, a fire, that is as completely effective as the fire in your living room fireplace, but is completely invisible. Well, at least it's invisible to the human eye.

Just as demonstrated with a microwave oven, there is an invisible fire that is completely known to the spirit world. The demons believe in Jesus and tremble at the thought of Him. They tremble at His name. They know that He is the One with eyes as of fire. They know Him as the One Who baptizes with fire while baptizing with the Holy Spirit. They have felt the scorch of His blaze, or at least seen their counterparts who have.

All things resonate at a given frequency. All things are frequency. Audio waves resonate at between 20 and 18,000 hertz. I remember from my days in electronics school that black and white TV signals (yes, there used to be such a thing) resonate at a different frequency than color TV. I won't try to quote the actual frequencies...it's been decades since I studied that. I was talking to a friend who used to work with NASA about this general subject and he said that microwave is loosely defined and generally refers to any signal whose speed is 1000 megahertz or higher. People also resonate at a given frequency. I always like to hear one of my favorite teachers and worship leaders say that Jesus knew at what frequency a particular wall was resonating, got in agreement with it, began to resonate in unison with it and walked right through it.

The point here is that all things resonate at a particular frequency. I believe spirits do as well...and **I believe there is a frequency or frequency spectrum that consumes spirit beings.** This explains in my mind how the fire of God destroys His enemies. When He has needed natural fire He has used it, as with Elijah at Mount Carmel. When He needs supernatural fire, to destroy an evil spirit, He knows exactly what frequency of fire to kindle and can do it instantly.

Supernatural fire is a Biblical idea. The most frequently used Hebrew word for "fire" in the Old Testament is the word "esh". The Blue Letter Bible online reference source, which uses Gesenius's Lexicon, gives "supernatural fire" as the second translation of "esh".[1] So the Bible acknowledges the existence of supernatural and natural fire-visible and invisible fire.

By the way, it is my belief that both visible and invisible fire resonate at frequency—and the different colors of fire at different frequencies. This is much like the colors of the rainbow, each color resonating at a different frequency until you get to ultra violet, which is invisible. This lets us *visualize* what I am describing here about an invisible realm. Some colors of the spectrum are visible and some are not. Some fire is visible and some is not.

So as you are reading this book, if any of it seems unrealistic, *just think microwave*, a clear demonstration of invisible fire.

On a Saturday in February of 2010, while I was in the process of writing this book, the Lord gave me a very real demonstration of the fact that there is a fire that is invisible and yet is still burning. I went outside and it was an overcast and cold morning. All that was

---

[1] "Hebrew Lexicon :: H784 (KJV)." Blue Letter Bible. Accessed 10 Jun, 2015. http://www.blueletterbible.org/lang/lexicon/lexicon.cfm?Strongs=H784&t=KJV.

missing was the snow. I felt so instantly drawn to build a fire in my chiminea. I hadn't planned on it...it was a sudden urge. I usually don't respond to those but it was Shabbat (Sabbath) and I was relaxing so I thought, why not. I thought I'd build a fire and sit and meditate and talk to the Lord a bit. As I began to light the fire and would touch the lighted match to the newspaper the fire would go out, instantly, as if someone or something was blowing it out. This happened three times, with three matches. I was about to get frustrated as I was lighting the fourth match and I noticed smoke coming from under the newspaper. Within a few seconds the paper ignited and was on fire. Now I've started several hundred fires in my lifetime but I've never noticed anything like this. I've never had the kindling blow out the fire before. The Lord grabbed my attention and let me know that He had orchestrated this whole ordeal— drawing me to start a fire—to demonstrate to me that even though my eyes cannot see it, there is a fire that burns and is effective that will accomplish His purpose. WOW!

The next chapter details the purpose of this book in giving the prayer strategy God has taught me and worked in me since 2007, and before. Let's look at this prayer and spiritual warfare strategy that is based upon a fire that is invisible to the human eye—the fire of God—the *Consuming Fire*!

> *"There is coming a day when God will judge His enemies little by little, one by one, and consume them with His fire...I believe we are at that day."*

Chapter 2

The Prayer Strategy

A Word of Caution: *Please read this book in it's entirety before engaging the enemy too deeply in the prayer strategy presented here. Chapter 11 is especially helpful in understanding how and when to use this strategy.*

In February of 2007 God began to speak to me and draw me into the prayer strategy that will be presented in this chapter. In reality, this is a warfare and deliverance strategy more than a prayer strategy. It is something I've learned under the direction of the Holy Spirit and by use: it is the most effective tool for seeing people set free I have ever experienced. This chapter contains the main purpose for this book. In this chapter I will detail this prayer or warfare strategy and how it came about in me, as well as give Scripture God has used to confirm what He's been teaching me. This will be framed from my understanding of the coming of God's Kingdom from a Biblical standpoint. I will discuss this from a topical approach rather than a Biblically chronological one.

I don't expect you to accept all that you read just from my stating it. I hope you won't do that. It is my desire that you study for yourself, especially Psalm 110, I Corinthians 15:24-26, Revelation 20 and Daniel 7:9-27. Please take some time to read and meditate on these passages asking Holy Spirit to teach you and confirm to you what you've read. Then, as He gives you the freedom, use these components in your own warfare. It is with this approach that faith will have grown in your being and you will enter another realm of the victory that Jesus has gained for us.

A little history.

When God began to give me the prayer and warfare strategy presented in this chapter I did not know all that I am presenting. I began to step into a new and unknown activity simply knowing that God was leading me into it. I would ask Him to confirm each new component to me. At first I thought this was a strategy just for me. I had been in a season of increased discernment for two years, from 2005 to 2007, and was more aware of evil around me than I had ever been. At times it was very frustrating and wearing mentally, emotionally and even spiritually (if that is possible). As God began to confirm this strategy to me using Scripture, I began to share it with other people, even teaching it on rare occasions. Since 2007 the Lord has confirmed the components of this prayer strategy on the fire of God, so that I now have ample Bible doctrine to share this with confidence, as well as use it for my own and other's deliverance and warfare.

As stated, in early 2007, I began to feel the Lord draw me into a desire to have the fire of God surround me to such a degree that whenever I sensed the presence of evil around me, it would be consumed. By that I mean that the spirit behind the evil I was sensing would be consumed. I even asked for personal ministry on at least two occasions, wanting prayer so that the fire of God would come on me and envelop me.

This desire for the fire of God in my life was confirmed and stirred in me even more when I was on a ministry trip to Guatemala and Mexico in March of 2007. One of our pastors and the leader of that trip, shared with our group from I Corinthians 3:12 that God wanted to, with His fire, consume everything about our lives that was wood, hay and stubble. I remember that, not because the teaching was new to me but because God was daily working it into my thinking.

During this time Holy Spirit began to draw me into the repeated act of binding the enemy and calling down the fire of God to consume it. I did this with what was at that time, huge results. After a short time my prayer changed...I began to "loose" the enemy, then bind, and then call down the fire of God on it. I did this because I didn't want to suffer the wrathful effects of the fire of God meant for the enemy. To use a modern military term, I didn't want to become "collateral damage", so I loosed the enemy off me and away from me before the fire of God came upon it. The strategy was honed even more when Holy Spirit began to instruct me to first bind the enemy, then loose, then call the fire of God down on it. He let me know that this was because the enemy, being spirit, was able to leave me in the instant I loosed it and attach itself to someone else before I could bind it. The enemy will become learned to this strategy and will try to evade the fire of God. So I needed to bind (limit the enemy's ability), then loose (the enemy from off me), then call down the fire of God on the enemy.

Though I have little Biblical proof as yet, I am convinced that spirit beings are like charges of electricity, to oversimplify it. Jesus said that He saw Satan <u>as lightening</u> fall from heaven. Jesus taught in Matthew 12:43 and Luke 11:24 that when an unclean spirit goes from someone it "walks through dry places" seeking rest. Dry places are always places of charges of static electricity. Another very strong proof of this to me is in the Greek word for "principality". The word is "arche". This is the same word used in English to describe an electric spark or charge that is dispensed. So many of our English words are just transliterations of words from Latin, Greek or Hebrew, and this word I believe is one of those. These are just three areas Biblically that lead me to believe what I've just stated about demons. However, the main point I'm making doesn't rest in this. My point is that spirit beings are not hampered by time and space and can move in an instant from one location, or person, to another, at least within their sphere of operation. That is one reason they need to be bound, to limit them from attaching themselves to someone after being loosed from their current victim. We see this type situation in Jesus' dealing with the Gadarene man possessed

27

with a legion demons in Matthew 8:28-34 and in Mark 5:1-17. The demons actually pled with Jesus to allow them to go into the heard of pigs when He evicted them from the man they had held captive.

If this whole scenario makes it seem as though I think spiritual forces are real entities, that's good. I do. They are! They have names. Throughout the Word of God we see demons, and angels for that matter, dealt with as though they are individual beings, called by names indicating their characteristics and purpose.

So, this is a brief history behind the prayer strategy presented here. There is a history behind this prayer strategy and this book. I'm reminded of II Corinthians 5:18. This has been one of my favorite verses for 30 years. It says that "all things are of God". So this part of my life that started to my knowledge in 2005 and continues, is of God, no matter how miserable it made me in the early days of my journey into it. This is a part of "His-story" in me!

The components of this prayer strategy.

The Lord has been teaching me the Scriptural reasoning behind the three main components of this "fire of God" prayer strategy. Those are:

1) Binding the enemy.

2) Loosing the enemy.

3) Calling down the fire of God to destroy the enemy.

I have for years known that God has given us the authority to bind and loose...anything. Matthew 16:19 and 18:18 teach this and it is very interesting that in these passages this doctrine is presented as a strategy for Kingdom dominion and prayer. I believe that those who take lightly or reject the ability Jesus gave us to bind and loose are greatly diminishing their power to do battle with the enemy and take Kingdom territory. They are very possibly putting themselves and those they associate with in danger. I have been totally amazed at the power of this simple act of faith and obedience to Jesus' teaching.

I have also heard people teach a very dogmatic doctrine of binding and loosing, even to almost condemn those who didn't use it "their way". I have studied these terms in detail. It is not my purpose to teach on this in detail in this book but suffice it to say that *Jesus gave us very broad authority* when He gave us this power to bind and loose.

The word for "bind" from the Greek text is "deo". It is translated in the Bible as to bind or be bound. Examples are to bind as in prison, with chains or chords, to bind sheaves in harvest, to tie as you would a colt or other animal, to bind as Satan would with an infirmity, to bind with grave cloths.[2]

The word for "loose" is *luo*. It means to unloose, as in loosening sandals. It is used to speak of breaking, as in one of the commandments, as though to be loosed from the authority of it. It is used of one loosing his ox from the stall, and of one being loosed from Satan's bondage of infirmity. It is translated "destroy" and used when Jesus said that the Pharisees could destroy the temple of His body and in three days He would raise it up. As a matter of fact, when I took Greek in college they called the year end vocabulary test the "Luo Test", as saying it would destroy you. With this definition, to loose would mean to destroy one's hold, authority or effect on another. It is used once in Acts as in a congregation breaking up or being released...loosed.[3]

Anything we bind on earth is bound in heaven and **anything** we loose on earth is loosed in heaven according to Jesus in Matthew 16:19. It says:

---

[2] "Greek Lexicon :: G1210 (KJV)." Blue Letter Bible. Accessed 10 Jun, 2015. http://www.blueletterbible.org/lang/lexicon/lexicon.cfm?Strongs=G1210&t=KJV

[3] "Greek Lexicon :: G3089 (KJV)." Blue Letter Bible. Accessed 10 Jun, 2015. http://www.blueletterbible.org/lang/lexicon/lexicon.cfm?Strongs=G3089&t=KJV

*"And I will give unto thee the keys of the kingdom of heaven: and **whatsoever** thou shalt bind on earth shall be bound in heaven: and **whatsoever** thou shalt loose on earth shall be loosed in heaven."*

Again, Matthew 18:18 gives the same quote from Jesus in a passage on the power of prayer and releasing, or not releasing, someone from their sin.

I have known for years that it is by the resurrection power of Jesus that we bind the enemy. However, Holy Spirit confirmed this to me Biblically by simply showing me it is Jesus' resurrection that conquered death and death is the strongest of His/our enemies. So, the ability to render the enemy powerless is related to the resurrection power of Jesus infused into His people (I Corinthians 15:26; Hebrews 2:14-16; Revelation 20:10-14).

When the angel binds Satan in Revelation 20:4 he no longer has the power to deceive. So we see that binding the enemy disables his deceptive power and the light of God can penetrate the minds of people he has deceived and give them the opportunity to chose to receive God and His truth (II Corinthians 4:4).

Loosing, related to demons, would lift them off of, or remove them from someone or some place. It could go as far as to remove them from a person's triune makeup, their spirit, soul and body.

For several months I had been using the strategy of calling down the fire of God and knowing that the enemy would be destroyed before I had a Scriptural foundation for this. I did it by faith that I was being led of the Holy Spirit, and <u>did I ever feel and know its power</u>. But this was simply an act of faith. Then one day the Lord allowed me to see Daniel 7, the river of fire that I was bathing in whenever I approached God's throne, and verse 26 which says that as the saints begin to take the Kingdom for the final and permanent time the enemy will be "consumed" and destroyed "unto the end". As I read this, I knew God was confirming to me with His written Word what I had been hearing Him say to my spirit...that He was going to use His fire to destroy the enemy little by little, one demon at a time, until the last enemy itself was destroyed-death. Then *Jesus, having worked through His saints* to conquer the Kingdom, would present it to the Father perfected and conquered forever (I Corinthians 15:24-26)!

So to summarize, this prayer strategy of the "fire of God" consists of binding the enemy, then loosing the enemy from off someone, then calling down the fire of God to destroy the enemy. Of 'course, we must first have discernment to know what spirit we are dealing with. This will be covered in detail in a later chapter.

God's Kingdom will come!

God's Kingdom is coming, and nothing can stop it. In reality God's Kingdom is here! It came in full force to the earth, contained in one man, when Jesus began

His earthly ministry. Luke 17:21 says, "...the Kingdom of God is within you." I have always, and still do, take that to mean that the Kingdom of God is within every believer. We can also see from various translations that this means His Kingdom is in the midst of us, corporately. When Jesus came He brought the Kingdom of God into the midst of God's people. Jesus said, *"...if I cast out devils by the Spirit of God, then the kingdom of God is come unto you."* (Matthew 12:28) And He did! The Kingdom had come! As God's people get our eyes opened and accept the reality of His Kingdom within us, and the resurrection power of Jesus within us, we will see His Kingdom invade earth in full force.

Nothing can stop God's Kingdom from coming, and from advancing into all the earth until the knowledge of God covers the earth as waters cover the sea (Isaiah 11:9; Habakkuk 2:14).

But how is God's Kingdom to advance?

Israel misunderstood God's Kingdom and missed their visitation as a result of their blindness. We cannot afford to have this happen to us, and yet the doctrines of God's Kingdom coming are as vast in the body of Christ as varieties in a sixteen bean soup. It is sad that many Bible loving believers avoid eschatology, the study of the end times, either out of fear or confusion. This is a temporary victory for the enemy since we, those same believers, are key to God's Kingdom filling the earth, the end result of "end time" doctrine.

God's Kingdom is coming...our eyes are being opened. The only reason that the Kingdom is not in operation now in full force in the earth, as it was in the life of Jesus where He walked, is that the body of Christ has not awakened to the victory Jesus wrought for us and the authority He imparted to us-His authority as Creator of the earth and Redeemer of the earth.

The Bible says that Jesus is now at the right hand of God and must sit there until His enemies become His footstool. It also says that He must reign until He has put all enemies under His feet. He is then going to present the Kingdom, having perfected it, to the Father. That is AWESOME! I love that. I heard a well known teacher describe it this way in his teaching: "The Father loved Jesus so much that He made the earth and gave it to Him and Jesus loved the Father so much that He redeemed the earth and gave it back to Him."

We see in God's Word that we are His army to subdue His enemies and conquer for Him and then to rule and reign with Him on the earth. This whole process will not be a fast one, at least by our standard of keeping time. As I see it, it will most likely take a thousand years. As God sees it, it will take a day.[4]

Jesus is expectantly waiting and watching for us to "take the Kingdom" so He can return while we are expectantly waiting and watching for his return so He

---

4 II Peter 3:8 (KJV)

34

can "take the Kingdom". At some point the two have to meet! They soon will... (This teaching is found in two places in the book of Hebrews. I'll discuss it later in the book.)

The "Kingdom Come" as I see it.
(*A topical chronology of God's Kingdom advance.*)

The following is an explanation or dissertation of God's Kingdom coming in the end times, as I see it Biblically. I call it a chronology of Kingdom advancement, not in Biblical order but in more of a topical order. As with anyone, our theology shapes our views and ultimately our practical living and our walk. I feel it is important to convey what I understand and believe about eschatology, the study of the end times, so that I can communicate properly what has been an amazingly effective prayer and warfare strategy in my life. This is because the destruction of the enemy is all about the establishment of God's Kingdom and vice versa, and this is what the "end times" are all about.

Jesus will establish His Kingdom in the midst of His enemies.

In Psalm 110 we see God tell Jesus to "rule in the midst of His enemies". Jesus, being always obedient to the Father, will and is doing just that. He started it in a physical, natural way when He came as a babe into human form. He started it even before that when He began to come upon the first human being with His Spirit, as the "Son of man", and work through human beings. He is now completing that ruling in the midst of His enemies by awakening His HUGE living army to their power in His name, through the power of His resurrection. He is awakening believers all over the world to who we are in Him and to the fact that He has given us dominion in the earth, and that this dominion in His name is greater than any force His enemy has.

Psalm 110:1 & 2 say:
> "The LORD said unto my Lord, Sit thou at my right hand, until I make thine enemies thy footstool. The LORD shall send the rod of thy strength out of Zion: rule thou in the midst of thine enemies."

Here God's command is to Jesus to, <u>from His right hand</u>, rule in the midst of His enemies until He makes them His footstool. I Corinthians bears this out in chapter 15. Verses 24 through 26 say:

> "Then comes the end, when He delivers the kingdom to God the Father, when

He puts an end to all rule and all authority and power. For He must reign till He has put all enemies under His feet. The last enemy that will be destroyed is death." (NKJV™)

It is so obvious to me from these passages that Jesus is in the process of reigning at God's right hand now. Hebrews 10:12 & 13 confirm this. He is, through His willing people, putting down one enemy and opposing authority after another, perfecting the Kingdom and taking over new dimensions of it, preparing it for the day He presents it to the Father. For most of my life I felt that Jesus would come back and, all at one time, put all opposing authority under His feet. I Corinthians 15 makes it clear that this will be a progressive task. The last enemy to be destroyed is death, the strongest of all God's enemies. This is also born out in Revelation 20:10-14 which show chronologically that death and hell are cast into the lake of fire after Satan himself, indicating they are stronger and last in the process. The fact that God deals with His enemies one at a time is a fairly common teaching in Scripture, as will be brought out in later chapters.

So, it is in the midst of Jesus enemies that He is establishing His Kingdom. ***We must have this mindset in order to operate in the mind of Christ.*** I think that many have been discouraged and intimidated in our trying to advance God's Kingdom because we failed to realize that Jesus' rule was "in the midst of His enemies". We've wanted them to roll over and play dead. Jesus wants us to act in His authority and they will play dead ultimately, though they won't be playing. (Remember, we're talking about spirit beings here.) And that's what this book is all about. They will first put up a fight...that's why it's called spiritual warfare.

Jesus will use you and me to establish His Kingdom.

The above statement is one of the most exciting things about the Kingdom of God to me. Jesus' intent, and the Father's intent, is for us to be the vessels that will carry out His dominion. He wants it that way. He is glorified in it that way. He created it to be that way. We see this in the earliest part of the Bible. Genesis 1:26-28 says:

> *"...Let Us make man in Our image, according to Our likeness; let them have dominion over the fish of the sea, over the birds of the air, and over the cattle, over all the earth and over every creeping thing that creeps on the earth. So God created man in His own image; in the image of God He created him; male and female He created them. Then God blessed them, and God said to them, "Be fruitful and multiply; fill the earth and subdue it; have dominion over the fish of the sea, over the birds of the air, and over every living thing that moves on the earth." (NKJV ™)*

Our having dominion is tied to our being created in God's image and likeness. God Rules! And God wants us to rule in and under Him. We see <u>God's creative purpose for man and woman</u> was for them to have <u>dominion</u> over every living thing that moves in the earth. That includes spirits, because they live and they move. God rules—an so should we—He meant it to be that way.

We see that Jesus came to earth to die and to restore the dominion that was lost when Adam and Eve sinned. Jesus is called the "last Adam" (I Corinthians 15:45), which is from a Hebrew word simply meaning the "last man". In other words, He came to show us how it's done! He came to be the ultimate demonstration of what God intended with man at creation. I Peter 4:11 says that it is through Jesus that *all praise and dominion* be for ever and ever. Amen! Yet in Genesis 1 we see that God gave man this dominion. In Psalm 8:1-6 we see the same thing, that God made us to have dominion and He has put all things under our feet. This involves silencing and stilling God's enemy and avenger. <u>It was God's creative purpose all along for us to rule this earth</u>. The first Adam messed it up and Jesus, the last Adam straightened it out and gave us back the authority to rule over all the earth, even authority to rule God's enemy in the earth. He did this by rightly aligning us with God again.

It has always been God's intent for us to take over and rule this earth as God's domain. "Kingdom" means...the King's domain. It is now time for that rule to take place, through us.

It is now time for Jesus' unlimited power to be displayed in and through the lives of His people. That's what Psalm 110:3 means when it says "Your people will be willing in the day of Your power." In other words, when the day comes for Jesus, who is sitting at the right hand of God ruling in the midst of His enemies, to have His power fully displayed, His people (you and I) will be willing to play our role. It is through us as willing participants that Jesus will exercise his power and dominion, His Kingdom rule. God's people are in the process of becoming so aware of our authority on earth and so fed up with the kingdom of darkness that we are becoming very willing participants.

There is one verse that makes it completely obvious to me that it is through you and me that God will bring all Jesus' enemies under His dominion. We have used the verses extensively in this book that state that Jesus is reigning at the right hand of God until all His enemies are made His footstool. The Apostle Paul got sight of how this would happen and wrote in Romans 16:20:

> *"And the God of peace shall bruise Satan under your feet shortly. The grace of our Lord Jesus Christ be with you. Amen."*

Here God makes it plain that it is through us, under our feet, we who are <u>the body</u> of Christ, that God will bruise Satan and subdue him under foot! This is why Daniel wrote in chapter 7 of his book that it is the saints who will take the Kingdom.

How will God's Kingdom come? Jesus will use you and me to establish His Kingdom.

Jesus will spend a 1000 year period taking, purging and perfecting His Kingdom.

I am talking briefly about the "end times", or eschatology...it is a necessary part of this book. After all, it is at the end of the ages that Jesus will have put down all evil and establish His as the Kingdom over all kingdoms. As I've stated, there are so many differing views on the end times that many believers avoid learning about and forming an opinion about end time teaching altogether. But I think it is important that we come to an understanding of what God has revealed about His Kingdom and the end times. There are many things He has chosen to keep hidden until His appointed time, but the one thing He makes very clear is that in the times of the end He will establish His Kingdom in the earth and that His saints will rule and reign with Him.

There is nothing quite as sad to me as a believer who is sitting back waiting to be "raptured out" and letting the enemy run rampant over them because they have been taught that we're just supposed to expect it to "wax worse and worse unto the end..." and saying,

"...Oh, Jesus, come and get me..." I like what I've heard Lance Wallnau say. He teaches that we should have an "occupation" mentality and theology and not an "evacuation" one. That fits what Jesus taught, and that is that we are to... occupy until He comes.[5] Occupy is a very interesting word. The root Greek word in Luke 19:13 is only used this one time in Scripture—it means to *carry on or conduct a business*, specifically *the business of a banker or trader*[6]. Merriam-Webster's dictionary gives the following definitions: *to live (in a house, etc...), to fill a place or space, to fill or use an amount of time, to take up a place, to take or hold possession or control of, to reside in as owner or tenant of.* The origin of the English word *occupy* comes from Latin words meaning to *take possession of, or seize.*[7] So from the above two sources we can paraphrase what Jesus taught when He said that we are to occupy until He comes: We are to invest what He's deposited into our lives to conduct His Kingdom business in a way that allows or causes us to seize and take possession of the territory He's assigned us, to fill it and control what goes on there, until He comes.

---

[5] Luke 19:13 (KJV)

[6] "Greek Lexicon :: G4231 (KJV)." Blue Letter Bible. Accessed 10 Jun, 2015. http://www.blueletterbible.org/lang/lexicon/lexicon.cfm?Strongs=G4231&t=KJV

[7] "Occupy." Merriam-Webster.com. Accessed June 10, 2015. http://www.merriam-webster.com/dictionary/occupy.

As a child I was exposed to much teaching on eschatology, or "the end times". Most of the modern day views I am at least somewhat familiar with, either because of my parent's teaching, my college training, or my personal study. I am more comfortable with my understanding of eschatology today than I have ever been, having tried to allow Holy Spirit to be my Teacher and shape my theology. He is still teaching me. What I have realized is that none of us know exactly how the end times will develop and what the establishment of God's Kingdom will look like. I also know that God has intentionally hidden some of this truth from us, until the time of the end, the time it is to be fulfilled (Daniel 12:9). I believe that some of the very teaching in this book is a

fulfillment of God's revealing some of the things that Daniel spoke of as hidden.

I also know this, that **the prayer strategy contained in this book is effective no matter what a person's end time theology is, when it is applied with faith.** I am living proof of this...I began knowingly living this prayer strategy in early 2007. I was at that time well into my journey <u>from</u> believing very strongly the pre-millennial, pre-tribulation or mid-tribulation rapture viewpoint. This strategy has been the most effective prayer and warfare tool I've ever seen and I have used it in the transition from where I was then to where I am now, a strong believer in what some call *Dominion Theology* (though there are varying degrees or definitions of that—as such, my view of Dominion Theology would differ from some views), working to see God's Kingdom established, waiting on Jesus' return and the transformational change into His likeness that Paul wrote about (I Corinthians 15:52).

I grew up in a home and in churches where we were taught that the world would get worse, Satan and darkness spread and take over, then Jesus would remove His church for a period of time and basically all hell would break loose on the earth. I now see clearly in Scripture that it is in the midst of His enemies that Jesus will enforce His Kingdom rule, and He will use us to do that. We are not escaping...**we are taking over!**

There are many Bible references to Jesus returning to earth and for His saints. In none of those passages do we ever see anything about us leaving earth for a time.

(I highly recommend the book *Victorious Eschatology*, by Harold Eberle and Martin Trench, to give a fresh and Biblical look at end time theology.)

In scripture I see a clear teaching about Jesus coming back and His saints being changed in a moment, in the twinkling of an eye. I Corinthians 15:51-58 teaches that the dead in Christ will rise with the trumpet sound and those who are still alive and know Christ will be changed with them into immortality. I Thessalonians 4:16-18 teaches that Jesus will descend from heaven, raise the dead in Christ and believers who are still alive will be caught up with them to meet Him in the air and "so shall we ever be with the Lord". In the many Bible references to Jesus returning to earth and for His saints, from all that I can see in Scripture, we are to serve Jesus fervently, accessing His full power which is available to us, "occupying till He comes". We are to take territory on earth for His Kingdom purposes, establishing His Kingdom and loosing the enemy's grip and strongholds. Then when Jesus comes He will change us into His glorified likeness, render us instantly sinless and incorruptible so that we can take territory and establish His Kingdom uninhibited by our own flesh. There is no evidence in the Bible that I can see that we are going anywhere...we are just going to be transformed into His likeness and then do what He created man to do in the beginning, rule this world in the image of God. I do believe in heaven...I believe it is a place Jesus is now preparing for us, where those who die in the Lord go to be with Him to await resurrection. And I believe it is coming down to earth some day at the end of the ages (John 14:2 & 3; Revelation 21:1 & 2).

I Thessalonians 4:16-17 says:

> "...*For the Lord himself shall descend from heaven with a shout, with the voice of the archangel, and with the trump of God: and the dead in Christ shall rise first: Then we which are alive [and] remain shall be caught up together with them in the clouds, to meet the Lord in the air: and so shall we ever be with the Lord.*"

If that meant we left earth then it would have to mean we would forever be gone from it. That is just not the teaching in God's Word. The Bible plainly teaches us that we will reign with Christ here on earth (Revelation 5:10), and in fact God's eternal city is coming "down" out of heaven, the new Jerusalem (Revelation 21:1-5). When Jesus comes the dead in Christ will arise, those who are alive in Christ will be changed into immortality, and we will in Jesus' full power spend what I believe is the balance of a thousand year period enforcing and spreading Jesus' Kingdom in the earth, until it covers the earth. In other words, we'll keep doing what we're to be doing now, just in a perfect and glorified state and with the devil bound so that he cannot deceive people (I Corinthians 15:52-58; Revelation 20:1-4).

Recent Christian teaching (within that last couple hundred years) has promoted a doctrine of something not ever mentioned in Scripture. There has been an evacuation mentality promoted among God's people and not an occupation mentality. *There has been a mentality of holding on until Jesus comes and takes us out rather than a mentality of taking over our sphere in Jesus' name and enforcing His Kingdom dominion.* Removing the obstacles to Kingdom dominion is what this book is given to.

There are many things about the end times that are hidden. Some are simply a blur. The Bible proves this in Daniel 12:9 which says that God told Daniel, "*...Go thy way, Daniel: for the words [are] closed up and sealed till the time of the end.*" One thing that is absolutely clear is that we are to advance God's Kingdom on earth and "occupy till Jesus' comes". Much popular end time teaching has for decades fought against our doing that as the body of Christ. It has taught us to win all the souls we can to Jesus and prepare them to be evacuated in the rapture, rather than getting people saved and training them to prepare earth for Jesus return, at which time He will rule all nations. God is in the process of revealing things about the end times now so that Christ's body can know how to move in power and authority and fulfill what He has destined. I have come to rest in the truth that God does not want me to know everything about the end times right now. The things I'm discussing here, however, are truths I am completely confident of regarding the end times.

Jesus will reign with His saints in an undisputed way, until His dominion is complete (Revelation 20:1-4).

Psalm 110 gives what I believe is a very clear overview of God's enforcing His Kingdom dominion. It begins by David quoting God as saying to Jesus, "...sit at My right hand until I make Your enemies Your footstool..." He then says, "Rule in the midst of Your enemies..." In other words, Jesus is now sitting at God's right hand. We know this because New Testament references tell He is sitting there right now (Romans 8:34; Colossians 3:1; Hebrews 10:12; 12:2; I Peter 3:22). He is to rule in the midst of his enemies. I always thought that Jesus was going to come and start His rule by destroying all His enemies. I was always taught that this was a trait of the "millennium", a time in which Jesus would reign for 1000 years of complete peace. I just assumed there would be no opposition to Him during His reign. Here in Psalm 110 we see something different. Jesus IS ruling, in the midst of enemies. We also see Jesus' people involved in this rule, the saints, you and me. Psalm 110:3 says, "...Your people shall be willing in the day of Your power..." So we see Jesus ruling from Heaven at the Father's right hand, and using His willing people to carry out this rule on earth. If Psalm 110 were all the Scripture I had on this I would be embellishing, but it is not, as we will see.

God tells Jesus in Psalms 110:1 to sit as His right hand until His enemies became His footstool. I Corinthians 15:25 says the Jesus must reign until His enemies be made His footstool. <u>So here we have a very clear picture of one piece of the end time puzzle.</u> Jesus is now at the right hand of God (Romans 8:34; Ephesians 1:20; Colossians 3:1; Hebrews 1:3). He will remain there until He has put all His enemies under His feet. Acts 3:20 & 21 solidify this teaching by stating that God will send Jesus again to earth after the "restitution (restoration) of all things", and that the heavens have received and are retaining him until such a time.

In Revelation 20 is another passage that talks about Jesus' reign and specifically the 1000 period man has called the Millennium. Here we see an angel coming with a great chain in his hand and *binding* Satan for 1000 years. During this time we, the saints, will rule under Jesus, Who is our High Priest after the order of Melchizedek. He has made us kings and priests in order that we may rule and reign with Him. Revelation 1:6 and 5:10:

> *"And hath made us kings and priests unto God and his Father; to him be glory and dominion for ever and ever. Amen...and hast made us unto our God kings and priests: and we shall reign on the earth."*

Coupling this with Revelation 20 we see that we will reign for the 1000 year period that Satan is chained. Revelation 20 gives more light on this part of the end time picture. We see the beginning of a 1000 year period of time when Satan will be bound by an angel with a great chain so that he cannot deceive the nations until this 1000 year period is over. I am aware that there are differences in understanding in the "millennium" or 1000 year period. Some believe this is a figurative term, equivalent to the phrase "God owns the cattle on a thousand hills". He obviously owns all the others, too. I believe the thousand year period is a literal millennium because of other teaching in the Word of God about numbers of years and days. God says that "...one day with the Lord is as a thousand years..." and vice versa (II Peter 3:8; Psalm 90:4). So let's just say "a day is coming" when Satan will be bound, cannot deceive, and God's saints will rule the earth. I believe that's what the Bible refers to as "the day of the Lord". Satan is called the one who weakens the nations (Isaiah 14:12). During this 1000 year period we see that Jesus will move through His saints to spread God's Kingdom to the nations, as we rule and reign with Him. The nations will turn to Jesus, their kings bow to His authority (Psalm 102:15; 138:4), and they will be delivered from the one who has weakened them (Isaiah 14:12).

Revelation 20:1-4 says:

> *"And I saw an angel come down from heaven, having the key of the bottomless pit and a great chain in his hand. And he laid hold on the dragon, that old serpent, which is the Devil, and Satan, and bound him a thousand years, And cast him into the bottomless pit, and shut him up, and set a seal upon him, that he should deceive the nations no more, till the thousand years should be fulfilled: and after that he must be loosed a little season. And I saw thrones, and they sat upon them, and judgment was given unto them: and [I saw] the souls of them that were beheaded for the witness of Jesus, and for the word of God, and which had not worshipped the beast, neither his image, neither had received [his] mark upon their foreheads, or in their hands; and they lived and reigned with Christ a thousand years. But the rest of the dead lived not again until the thousand*

years were finished. This [is] the first resurrection."

This picture makes it clear that Jesus will begin a 1000 year period of reigning in which Satan will be bound, the nations will not be deceived and the light of the glorious Gospel of Christ will have free course for the global harvest to come in to the body of Christ and be reaped. *Jesus will spend a 1000 year period taking, purging and perfecting His Kingdom.*

We will be a part of that reign. Those who have died as believers in Jesus at this time will be raised from the dead. I believe that we will all be a part of the binding of Satan because we have been given authority in the earth to bind "whatsoever". "Whatsoever" is a word that is both about things and people. It comes from a Greek word which is translated "whosoever" as well as "whatsoever". The body of Christ is coming nearer and nearer a corporate level of faith for this to take place, though we have quite a way to go yet. The day will come when we will reach that faith level and the angel will be sent to bind Satan and the 1000 year period known as the millennium will begin.

When Revelation 20 is contrasted to I Corinthians 15 it becomes obvious that we, under Jesus, will spend 1000 years putting down all forces that oppose Jesus' reign as King. I Corinthians 15:24-26 teach that Jesus must reign until He has put all enemies under His feet. Death will be the last enemy destroyed. At the end of the one thousand year reign of Jesus with His saints, Satan will be released from his enchainment so that he can deceive those who have still rejected Jesus as Lord of their lives (II Thessalonians 2:7-12)...Jesus will then destroy both Satan and those who have willingly allowed him to deceive them. We see this in Revelation 20:8 & 9. We also see here that death and hell are cast into the lake of fire, at the end of a list of others that are cast into this fire. Jesus will then present the Kingdom to the Father having conquered every foe. (This is the combined teaching of I Corinthians 15 and Revelation 20).

In chapter 7 of his book, Daniel gives us his prophetic picture of this scene. I will discuss it later, below.

So let's summarize these thoughts:

> A. Jesus is now reigning at the right hand of God.
> B. He has to stay there until all His enemies are put under His feet.
> C. A 1000 year period is coming in which Satan will be bound and not allowed to deceive the nations, or blind them.
> D. In this period of time we, the saints of God, will reign with Jesus in resurrection bodies and enforce His Kingdom authority.
> E. At the end of this time Satan will be released for a short season.
> F. Then Satan, death and hell will be destroyed.

G. Jesus will present the Kingdom to the Father having conquered every enemy and perfected the Kingdom.

H. At this time the prophecies of Revelation 21 and 22 will be fulfilled and God will dwell with us and in us in a new heaven and on a new earth forever.

I realize this seems so foreign to much of our traditional end time theology, but it is written in the Bible and has been since the cannon was complete.

What about "the Rapture"?

I believe the day is coming when the trumpet of God will sound and Jesus will descend from heaven in such power that those of us in Christ, even the dead, will be lifted to meet Him. I believe this will be with such full manifestation of the Light of God that Jesus possesses that we will be imprinted with His image and changed into His likeness, much like an image is imprinted on film when the flash of a camera light hits it through the film. We will be changed into His likeness and do His Kingdom business just as He would do it—perfectly.

As much as I'd like to believe that what I was taught as a child (that the rapture would happen and we'd all as believers be caught up off the earth and escape all the evil of this world and it's punishment) the teaching that God's people will be missing from earth for a time to allow God's enemy to run rampant is totally missing from Scripture. The closest thing to that teaching I can find is in 2 Thessalonians 2:1-10, giving a scenario in which the wicked one is being withheld from "all deceivableness of unrighteousness" till whatever is restraining the wicked one is taken out of the way. Many have surmised that to be the church indwelled by Holy Spirit. This could be true, but it could also be true that we, the church, right here on earth, just stop restraining the wicked one by our prayer, intercession and decree. We do hold this authority in Jesus' name. It is definitely true that we the saints, in our role as intercessors at the throne, are the ones who are responsible for God pouring the vials of judgment onto the earth as seen in the book Revelation. This can be done from the earth or present with God in heaven, bodily. The Word of God is clear that we as God's people gather around His throne from our position here on the earth, and that we are seated with Jesus now in the heavenly place in our spirits.

My point of discussion here is that I do not see anywhere in Scripture the teaching that God's people are going to be taken away from the earth. God made man to enforce His authority in the earth. Jesus came and died to redeem it and save it (Luke 19:10). God doesn't want us vacating earth but occupying it. As to the wrath to come upon those who reject God, His Word and His Son, I am fully convinced that Psalm 91 is true and that God is able and willing to cover and protect us from anything that is being poured out upon this earth on wickedness. God has an extreme desire and willingness to hide us in His pavilion. Proverbs chapter one gives much attention to this teaching.

It has been very interesting to me to learn recently that our founding church fathers did not believe in a rapture. It was not until very recently in history that such a teaching became common in the church. The spread of the rapture teaching greatly coincides with the popularity of the Scofield Study Bible. There is much historical documentation about this. Again, the book Victorious Eschatology by Harold Eberle and Martin Trench give some very good insight on this.

My main and greater point is that the prayer strategy laid out in this book works no matter what your eschatology. We are not to hide—you and I are not to hide from the enemy but to engage and uproot the enemy. We are to dislodge and remove the enemies strongholds and allow the Kingdom of God to come and be established.

Jesus is coming back.

Jesus is coming back. He is coming in fire. He is returning to take vengeance on His enemies (II Thessalonians 1:8). And when He comes you and I as believers will be changed into His likeness and immortality to enforce and carry out His Kingdom, the King's Domain, in the earth.

Jesus will put His enemies down one at a time or little by little until He reigns unopposed.

Most of us people have a common trait...we don't like to take on too much adversity at one time. Many people put off responsibility; they procrastinate, because responsibility sometimes carries adversity. Other than the tendency to totally ignore responsibility, this is not necessarily a bad thing. As a matter of fact, it is fairly common in the Word of God to find that God handles adversity one element, or one opponent, at a time. In Exodus 23:30 and Deuteronomy 7:22, we see this principle in God's dealing with Israel's opponents. This will be discussed in more detail later. God told Israel He would drive their enemies out of their promised land little by little, even one at a time.

This should be very encouraging to us. This makes the task of Kingdom dominion much more manageable and easier—I like *easy*.

I think God enjoys dealing with His enemies one at a time. He certainly could destroy them all at once if He wanted to. But I think He gets more glory and pleasure out of doing it one at a time. He can take His time and watch His enemies wallow in defeat. He can watch the fear of God spread from one enemy to another as they know their time is coming. He actually laughs, makes sport, mocks at His enemy in their demise (Psalm 2:4; 37:13; Proverbs 1:22-33).

In regard to the body of Christ taking Kingdom territory one place at a time, and dislodging one enemy at a time, we see this principle in the Word of God in places other than Exodus and Deuteronomy. In I Corinthians 15 we find that there is a progression of the enemy's destruction and that *the last enemy to be destroyed* will be death. I Corinthians 15:24-26 says:

> *"Then cometh the end, when he shall have delivered up the kingdom to God, even the Father; when he shall have put down all rule and all authority and power. For he must reign, till he hath put all enemies under his feet. The last enemy that shall be destroyed is death."*

This is a teaching that, though veiled to the casual reader, becomes clear when looked at more closely: the destruction of God's enemy will be gradual and I believe in the order of the strength of the enemy, the weakest being destroyed first, and so on.

Psalm 110:1 together with I Corinthians 15:25 gives more confirmation of the gradual destruction of God's enemies. Let me put these two verses together so we can see a fuller picture.

> *"... The LORD said unto my Lord, Sit thou at my right hand, until I make thine enemies thy footstool...For He must reign, till He hath put all enemies under His feet."*

57

Scripture makes it obvious that Jesus will sit at the right hand of God <u>until</u> He has put all enemies under His feet. In fact, Psalm 110:1 is repeated verbatim in Matthew 22:44, Mark 12:36 and Hebrews 1:13. He wants us to know that Jesus is at His right hand until the job is finished, so He established it in the mouth of three witnesses. Jesus must reign until all enemies are put under His feet. Then He will present the Kingdom to the Father forever. This is the amazing message of I Corinthians 15:24-26.

There is yet another confirmation of the gradual conquering and dominion of Jesus over His enemies. Acts 3:21 says the heavens "must receive" Jesus until the times of restitution of all things. "Restitution" is a word that indicates a time process. It comes from the word "restore" and to restore something takes time. Jesus is restoring all things to Himself through the saints of God. I believe when this restoration process is complete we will see the earth restored to the place it was when given to Adam to care for, before the fall of man. Hebrews 2:8 probably describes the current state of the Kingdom better than any description I've read. It says:

> *"Thou hast put all things in subjection under his feet. For in that he put all in subjection under him, he left nothing [that is] not put under him. But now we see not yet all things put under him."*

In other words, God has put all things under Jesus' feet, but we don't <u>see</u> that yet, because we are in the process of learning of our authority given to us by Jesus and then using it to bring His enemies into submission to Him. As we do so, one enemy or stronghold at a time, we see one territory at a time restored to Jesus. At some point we as the body of Christ will come into the knowledge of how to sustain these spheres of dominion and maintain Kingdom control of areas conquered, until ultimately the whole earth is "restored" back to the rule of Jesus. I believe the strategy presented in this book is a part of the process of Kingdom possession and maintenance.

Jesus will work through His saints to subdue His enemies and restore all things.

Certain passages in the Word of God are plain that it is the saints of God who will take the Kingdom, and that Jesus will rule and reign forever and ever. Daniel 7 is *such an incredible passage*. Verses 21, 22, 25 and 27 say the following:

> *"I beheld, and the same horn made war with the saints, and prevailed against them; Until the Ancient of days came, and judgment was given to the saints of the most High; and the time came that the saints possessed the kingdom...And he shall speak [great] words against the most High, and shall wear out the saints of the most High, and think to change times and laws: and they shall be given into his hand until a time and*

> *times and the dividing of time...And the*
> *kingdom and dominion, and the*
> *greatness of the kingdom under the*
> *whole heaven, shall be given to the*
> *people of the saints of the most High,*
> *whose kingdom [is] an everlasting*
> *kingdom, and all dominions shall serve*
> *and obey him.*

We see here a battle, and clearly the saints of the Most High God winning the battle, taking the Kingdom of God, and then it being His Kingdom for ever.

God will work through His saints to conquer Kingdom territory on earth. After all, it was to man—Adam—that God gave earthly dominion in the first place. And it was Jesus, the 'last Adam', that came to restore that dominion...to man, on earth.

In the book of Revelation we see that authority will be given to the saints of God to rule and reign with Jesus. Revelation 5:10, 20:6 and 22:5 state the following:

> *(You have)...made us unto our God*
> *kings and priests: and we shall reign on*
> *the earth... Blessed and holy [is] he that*
> *hath part in the first resurrection: on*
> *such the second death hath no power,*
> *but they shall be priests of God and of*
> *Christ, and shall reign with him a*
> *thousand years...And there shall be no*
> *night there; and they need no candle,*

*neither light of the sun; for the Lord
God giveth them light: and they shall
reign for ever and ever.*

II Timothy repeats a theme that runs throughout the
New Testament when it says that if we suffer with
Christ we will also reign with Him. If we deny Him He
will deny us.

As we awaken to the authority we have in Jesus
Christ we truly come back into the dominion rule God
gave us in Genesis 1:26 & 28 and in Psalm 8:6 which
says:

*"Thou madest him to have dominion
over the works of thy hands; thou hast
put all [things] under his feet..."*

It IS through the saints of the Most High God that He
will retake the Kingdom, enforce Kingdom dominion
and restore His reign in the earth.

Jesus' Kingdom will be taken, purged and perfected, through the saints, by fire.

It is by fire that the Lord will take the Kingdom. This is
made very clear in Daniel 7. We will look at it shortly.
First, let me say that I Corinthians 3:11-15 makes it
clear that all things, or at least "every man's work", will
be tried with fire. That which endures the fire is eternal
and it is gold, silver and precious stones. That which

is consumed is of a sort that will not endure the fire and therefore is not lasting, not eternal.

In Isaiah 66[8] God tells us that He is coming with fire to carry out His Kingdom and covenant purpose, and that <u>He will plead with all flesh by fire and by the sword</u>.

Amos 7:4 says that the Lord will "contend" by fire. The word contend is a word that means He will strive as with words. This is the same picture Daniel gives as the Ancient of Days takes His throne and sits in judgment on the kingdoms of the earth, including antichrist's kingdom.

Let's now look at Daniel 7. This chapter gives a clear picture of the throne of God, Whom he calls the Ancient of Days. God's throne is presented as being an environment of fire. Daniel 7: 9 & 10 says:

> *"I beheld till the thrones were cast down, and the Ancient of days did sit, whose garment was white as snow, and the hair of his head like the pure wool: his throne was like the fiery flame, and his wheels as burning fire. A fiery stream issued and came forth from before him: thousand thousands ministered unto him, and ten thousand times ten thousand stood before him:*

---

8 Isaiah 66:16 (KJV)

the judgment was set, and the books were opened."

This is the same scenario we find in Revelation 5 where John wrote:

"And I beheld, and I heard the voice of many angels round about the throne and the beasts and the elders: and the number of them was ten thousand times ten thousand, and thousands of thousands..."

Then, with the saints worshipping in the river or stream of fire preceding from God's throne, Daniel 7:18-26 completes the picture. He says that the saints of the Most High God shall take the Kingdom and possess it forever and ever upon the seating of the Ancient of Days on His throne of fire, and that the enemy and his dominion will be *"consumed and destroyed unto the end."*

So it is by fire that we take the Kingdom. God is the consuming fire. Jesus is the baptizer in the fire. As we approach the throne of God in worship we are stepping into God's river, of living water and also of fire. As we do, Jesus baptizes us in the river of fire as we surrender our lives to Him.

Jesus is making us vessels of his fire.

As Jesus baptizes us in the river of fire He is making us flaming torches—vessels to carry the fire of God into the earth to consume God's enemy and to possess the Kingdom, one territory at a time. This is why both Psalm 104:4 and Hebrews 1:7 say that God makes His ministers a flame of fire. In both scriptures, Hebrew and Greek, the root word for "ministers" is a word used repeatedly to describe human beings who are ministers in flesh and blood. I say this to prove that God is not just talking about angels or spirit beings in these two verses. It is God's intent, His eternal plan, to make us a consuming fire to carry out His desire that all things be purified in the Refiner's fire and that His spiritual enemies be destroyed by fire (Malachi 3:2; Psalm 37:20; 104:4; Hebrews 1:7).

We Are To Occupy Now!

Jesus told us to "occupy till He comes" (Luke 19:11-13). He gave this command two thousand years ago in the parable of the nobleman and his ten servants. His obedient disciples have been carrying out that command and mission for two thousand years with the knowledge and faith they have had to do so. As God has unfolded more light to succeeding generations, that generation of believers has been accountable to "occupy" Kingdom territory to a new level of faith and knowledge. One internationally known teacher and bishop over hundreds of local churches talks a lot about the concept of "present truth", based upon II Peter 1:12. He describes this as the teaching that God is in the process of unfolding or revealing truth, already contained in Scripture but hidden to past generations of believers. As we get new truth revealed from God's Word we become accountable to walk in that revelation. New knowledge carries with it a new level of faith to accomplish things previous generations have not been able to accomplish. God will continue this "present truth" revelation process "until we all come into the knowledge of the faith of the Son of God and the full stature of the measure of Christ" (Ephesians 4:13).

The reason I write this section is that I am aware I'm writing about a concept God will use in the body of Christ during what many have called "the millennium". I will call it the day when the Kingdom of God is in full fruition and being realized upon the earth. In that day God will be in the process of devouring His enemies one at a time with His all-consuming fire. However, once we get this truth revealed to us and our eyes are opened, we should not wait until we see the "millennium" come upon earth. This is true because none of us know when that day will be and exactly what it will look like. One internationally known pastor from California, said recently that we could so tap into the heart of God and reach a level of faith that we are actually experiencing things we have thought were reserved for the "millennium". This is exactly what David did with the Tabernacle of David. He so captured the heart of God and His passion for His saints to live in the state of worship around the throne that David ushered Israel into an age that was reserved for the post crucifixion and resurrection age, after the veil in the temple was rent in two from top to bottom and the saints had access through Jesus' blood to the throne of God (Matthew 27:51; Mark 15:38; Hebrews 4:14-16).

When Jesus gave the command to "occupy till He comes" it was to begin at that moment. He was speaking reality and imparting the faith to make it happen. When God said, "...the enemies of the Lord shall be consumed into smoke..." (Psalm 37:20), He was speaking reality and imparting the faith to carry it out. He was speaking present truth. It's just that some of us are only now getting our eyes opened to this truth.

Let all of us as God's people take up, or intensify, the business of taking and occupying Kingdom territory. It is with the fire of God that this is accomplished. To that end this book is written, so please continue reading, to the end...

Eternal Punishment from the Presence of the Lord!

As I was finishing this book I sensed a need to address a concern I've had—that is that readers will think that I do not believe in the eternal aspect of punishment in hell fire. Let me be clear that I do.

I have realized that someone could think that because I am addressing the "annihilation" of demonic spirits that I do not believe in eternal punishment in hell. I do firmly believe in that. I do not have the answer yet to what could be construed as a contradiction that occurs when you say the fire of God will destroy God's enemies and also that hell is eternal punishment. I do believe both to be true.

I can best leave this to be addressed by II Thessalonians 1:8 & 9 which says that God will...

> *"In flaming fire taking vengeance on them that know not God, and that obey not the gospel of our Lord Jesus Christ: Who shall be <u>punished with everlasting destruction</u> from the presence of the Lord, and from the glory of his power..."*

As is obvious here, there is an everlasting destruction which is based in the fire of God. When the time comes that God has determined for one of His enemies to be destroyed, then His fire will envelop that enemy and an eternal destruction process will have begun. WE ARE A PART OF THAT PROCESS IN GOD'S ETERNAL PLAN.

A word of caution!

One word of clarification and caution here...this book is dedicated to the doctrine of God's intent to destroy

His enemies by fire. These enemies are spiritual...they are spirits-demons, and Satan himself. However, flesh and blood can get caught in this. The only way flesh gets caught in this and is harmed or destroyed is if it remains in a state of "enmity" with God. If someone chooses to rebel against God, His process of fire and the purpose for His fire, they could be harmed or even destroyed. All wickedness someday will be destroyed. (The root of the Hebrew word for *wickedness really means* or indicates *misalignment*.) That means spirits as well as people who have been wrongly aligned under God and rejected His mercy. I spoke earlier of "collateral damage" from the fire of God. Other than the above description of destruction upon flesh which has rejected God's plan, it is my opinion that the only collateral damage that would occur is in a case where someone would try to enforce God's fire on a structure without the proper level of faith and out of proper time. When we access the fire of God, it consumes, and it consumes everything that is not eternal. This means that temporal things in our lives are subject to be consumed. That's one reason that it is very important to walk in God's timing when we engage the enemy using the fire of God. As we approach God's presence His fire affects everything about us. When God sees things in our lives that are not going into eternity with us He handles the consumption of them in His grace and mercy. We need to act the same way, and the way we do that is to walk in faith and God's timing is the use of His fire in warfare.

Please read this book in its entirety before engaging the enemy too deeply in the prayer strategy presented here. Chapter 11 is especially helpful in understanding how and when to use this strategy.

Summary!

Though I've stated it above in this chapter, I want to summarize the chapter and the prayer strategy for clarity.

> By the authority we have been given through Jesus' resurrection power, we can bind any demon we sense at work in any life or territory we are called to operate or minister in. We can then loose that spirit by the Sword of the Spirit, the Word of God, to lift it off of the people or places affected by it. If we sense that God has given faith and that the time for the destruction of that demonic power has come, we can call down the fire of God to consume it.

This is the *consuming fire* prayer strategy that this book is written to explain. I've been using this strategy and growing in the knowledge of it since early 2007 and can testify that this is a tremendously effective strategy. I encourage you to begin to use this and let the Holy Spirit develop your faith in this realm (Again, after reading this entire book).

In reality, we are carriers of the very fire of God. It is my belief and contention in this book that this fire in us and on us is for, not a state of temporary deliverance, but the annihilation of a given spirit[9]. That doesn't mean that another like spirit cannot come, especially if a door is opened to it. I do mean though, that the particular spirit being dealt with is destroyed. We must have faith strong enough to operate on this level. We will deal with this in detail in a later chapter. Be very cautious in exercising this authority. It is my belief that principalities will be the last to be destroyed in a region, and that this will come by a corporate effort of the church, the body of Christ in a territory. One can come into some serious circumstances and danger by engaging the enemy at this level prematurely. Please make sure you've read the chapter on "Judge nothing before it's time." Ask the Lord to give you the understanding He wants you to have before you engage in this strategy.

Hebrews 10:13 says that Jesus now sits at the right hand of God "expecting" till his enemies are made His footstool. Hebrews 9:28 says that to those who "look" for Jesus, He will appear to them without sin unto salvation. The interesting thing here is that the words "expecting" and "look" in these two verses come from the same Greek root word, and they can both be translated the same way according to Strong's Concordance. When I saw this, I realized that the body of Christ has been down here waiting on Jesus to come back and rescue us while Jesus Himself has

---

[9] Daniel 7:26 (NASB)

been seated on His throne waiting on us to submit to Him, "being willing in the day of His power", and help Him conquer and destroy the enemy and possess the Kingdom for Him. As I stated earlier, Jesus is expectantly waiting and watching for us to "take the Kingdom" so He can return while we are expectantly waiting and watching for his return so He can "take the Kingdom". At some point the two have to meet! They soon will...

I want to include a list of Scriptures that prove that with fire God will destroy His enemies, and that we play a role in that.

God's fire will ultimately consume all His enemies, and all wickedness from the earth (Ps. 104:35). **I love that statement!** Below are some Scriptures that prove this. Some of these have been used elsewhere in this book, but I wanted to compile them here just for emphasis and to make it evident that this was the purpose and plan of God. Here is the list:

> **Psalm 9:6-8, 17:** *"O thou enemy, <u>destructions are come to a perpetual end</u>: and thou hast destroyed cities; their memorial is perished with them. But the LORD shall endure for ever: he hath prepared his throne for judgment. And he shall judge the world in righteousness, he shall minister judgment to the people in uprightness...The wicked shall be*

turned into hell, [and] all the nations that forget God."

Psalm 11:6: "Upon the wicked he shall rain snares, fire and brimstone, and an horrible tempest: [this shall be] the portion of their cup."

Psalm 18:37: "I have pursued mine enemies, and overtaken them: neither did I turn again till they were consumed."

Psalm 21:8 & 9: "Thine hand shall find out all thine enemies: thy right hand shall find out those that hate thee. Thou shalt make them as a fiery oven in the time of thine anger: the LORD shall swallow them up in his wrath, and the fire shall devour them."

Psalm 37:20: "But the wicked shall perish, and the enemies of the LORD [shall be] as the fat of lambs: they shall consume; into smoke shall they consume away."

Psalm 68:2: "As smoke is driven away, [so] drive [them] away: as wax melteth before the fire, [so] let the wicked perish at the presence of God."

Psalm 97:3: *"A fire goeth before him, and burneth up his enemies round about."*

Psalm 104:35: *"Let the sinners be consumed out of the earth, and let the wicked be no more. Bless thou the LORD, O my soul. Praise ye the LORD."*

Daniel 7:9,10,11, 26: *"I beheld till the thrones were cast down, and the Ancient of days did sit, whose garment [was] white as snow, and the hair of his head like the pure wool: his throne [was like] the fiery flame, [and] his wheels [as] burning fire. A fiery stream issued and came forth from before him: thousand thousands ministered unto him, and ten thousand times ten thousand stood before him: the judgment was set, and the books were opened. I beheld then because of the voice of the great words which the horn spake: I beheld [even] till the beast was slain, and his body destroyed, and given to the burning flame... But the judgment shall sit, and they shall take away his dominion, to consume and to destroy [it] unto the end."*

I Corinthians 3:13-15: *"Every man's work shall be made manifest: for the day shall declare it, because it shall be revealed by fire; and the fire shall try every man's work of what sort it is. If any man's work abide which he hath built thereupon, he shall receive a reward. If any man's work shall be burned, he shall suffer loss: but he himself shall be saved; yet so as by fire."*

Revelation 20: 10, 14 & 15: *"And the devil that deceived them was cast into the lake of fire and brimstone, where the beast and the false prophet [are], and shall be tormented day and night for ever and ever. And death and hell were cast into the lake of fire. This is the second death. And whosoever was not found written in the book of life was cast into the lake of fire."*

These are but a few. There are *many more* Bible passages that prove God's intent to destroy His enemies with fire.

So in summary:

* We have the authority to bind, then loose and then call down the fire of God to destroy spiritual evil, or evil spirits.
* Jesus will establish His Kingdom in the midst of His enemies.

74

* Jesus will use you and me to establish His Kingdom in the midst of His enemies.
* Jesus will spend a 1000 year period taking, purging and perfecting His Kingdom.
* Jesus will put His enemies down one at a time or little by little until He reigns unopposed.
* Jesus will work through His saints to subdue His enemies and restore all things.
* Jesus' Kingdom will be taken, purged and perfected, through the saints, by fire.
* Jesus is making us vessels of His fire.
* We are not to wait to begin to occupy Kingdom territory for God.

*I have really put myself at risk relationally in writing this book. I've done it because I want others to know the same power in war, relief and deliverance that I've known and am still learning about. Mainly, I've done it because the Lord put it in my heart and has confirmed to me that I was to do so. **PLEASE READ** the balance of this book. I believe this book contains one of the strategies that the Father will use in uprooting the enemy, destroying evil and establishing His Kingdom. <u>Each following chapter supports and explains</u>*

<u>what is contained in this chapter and in the prayer strategy on the fire of God.</u>

"*There is coming a day when God will judge His enemies little by little, one by one, and consume them with His fire...I believe we are at that day.*"

Chapter 3

Jesus, a Consuming Fire!

God is a consuming fire. Jesus is the express image of the Father, so He is also a consuming fire. He said to His disciples, "...if you have seen me you have seen the Father..." Hebrews 1:3 says that Jesus is the exact character of the Father. The verse reads, *"(Jesus) being the brightness of His glory, and the express image of his person, and upholding all things by the word of his power, when he had by himself purged our sins, sat down on the right hand of the Majesty on high..."* The words "express image" are from the Greek word "charaktar". This word is only used in the entire New Testament one time, in Hebrews 1:3. When God decided to describe Jesus He chose to use a word that we have come to admire. Jesus is the replica of the Father, the exact reproduction, the express image, the exact *character*, possessing the exact characteristics of the Father. (The Greek word used is *charakter*, with a long e sound.)

So, Jesus is also a consuming fire, because God is. Take a look at the biblical descriptions of Jesus related to fire:

Jesus has eyes of fire. We see this presented in Revelation 1:14 which says, *"His head and his hairs were white like wool, as white as snow; and his eyes were as a flame of fire;"* Revelation 2:18 and Revelation 19:12 also tell us that Jesus' eyes are eyes of fire.

Jesus is going to baptize with fire. We as Christians have been consumed for centuries with Jesus' baptizing us with His Holy Spirit, as well we should be. But that same teaching is tied to His baptizing us with fire. Matthew 3:11 and Luke 3:16 both teach us that Jesus will baptize us with fire. I believe this is to burn up any chaff in our lives and around us. He wants us to be purged of anything that will keep us from being productive in His Kingdom purpose for us. This is very similar to what we see in I Corinthians 3, where all our works will be tried by fire and only what is gold, silver and precious stone will be preserved, and it will be purified and beautified.

Jesus descended into hell but was not hurt by the fire, nor consumed by it (Ephesians 4:9).

Jesus was the fourth man in the fire with the three Hebrew children, not being consumed or hurt by the fire while also protecting and delivering them from the fire (Daniel 3:25).

We will all appear before the judgment seat of Christ where all our life's work will be tried by fire (Romans 14:10; II Corinthians 5:10; I Corinthians 3:13).

Jesus stated that He came to send or scatter fire on the earth. We find this in Luke 12:49 and 50. This same passage seems to teach that Jesus was to be baptized Himself with fire. We'll look at that further later in the book, but the point here is that Jesus said He came to start a fire in the earth.

Jesus will destroy His enemies with the brightness of His coming. II Thessalonians 2:8 says, *"And then shall that Wicked be revealed, whom the Lord shall consume with the spirit of his mouth, and shall destroy with the brightness of his coming..."* This is tied to Psalm 97:3 which says that a fire goes before Him and burns up all His enemies. This is also related to Daniel 7 and the wheels of fire under God's throne. God showed me that this is because His Kingdom is in advance. His throne is conquering as we, His saints, take on our role on earth. It may very well be that we are the wheels under His throne, advancing His Kingdom into all dominions on earth. As you read the rest of this manuscript you will get a fuller picture of why I say this and just what I mean by it.

All the above mentions of fire related to Jesus have their own measure of depth that I will not attempt to deal with right now. I'm sure there are many more Biblical references to fire related to Jesus that we could mention, but these are enough to make us aware that fire is a major component of Jesus purpose and ministry on the earth, at least in the spirit realm.

Jesus, the express image of the Father and fullness of the Godhead bodily, is a consuming fire, as God is a consuming fire.

That being the case, it becomes obvious that He wants to make us into a consuming fire, since He is fashioning us into His image.

Please read on…

"There is coming a day when God will judge His enemies little by little, one by one, and consume them with His fire…I believe we are at that day."

Chapter 4

Jesus Promised He Would Baptize Us With Fire

Why did Jesus promise to baptize us with fire and the Holy Spirit? Could it be because there are two rivers flowing from the throne of God? Or is there just one river, with two components, fire and water? We'll deal with this more later in the book, but for now let me just say that this is seen in Revelation 22:1 and Daniel 7:9 & 10. The Holy Spirit is represented by fire and by water. He is the living water of John 7:37-39 where Jesus said out of our inner most being would flow rivers of living water if we believe on Him. Holy Spirit is the fire on the seven golden candlesticks in Revelation 1:4-2:1.

These are very deep and great thoughts to be pursued, but not my purpose here. In this writing my assignment is to pursue an emphasis on the fact the Jesus will immerse us in fire. This is associated with His baptizing us in the Holy Spirit (Matthew 3:11; Luke 3:16). It is most likely true that when Jesus baptizes us in the Holy Spirit He is immersing and surrounding us in fire. The more we are baptized in the Holy Spirit the more we are immersed in the fire of God. The more this happens the more purified we become, as He purges all about us that is eternal and consumes all about us that is of this world—temporal or temporary.

I have long believed that the baptism of the Holy Spirit was not to be a one time occurrence, but rather to happen over and over. The imparting of the indwelling Holy Spirit is a one time occurrence which happens at salvation, but Jesus wants us to be immersed in His Holy Spirit often, even daily. We don't take the attitude that, "I bathed last month...I don't need to bathe again this week." Neither should we take the attitude that we were baptized in the Holy Spirit once...we don't need that any more. As we grow in grace and the knowledge of Jesus, we are delivered from more and more of flesh and have more room for Holy Spirit to possess us, so we need to be baptized in Him often. As we are, we are baptized in the fire of God and He purges us more and more into His instrument of fire... His burning ember.

It is interesting that when we approach the throne of God we are actually stepping into His river of fire flowing from His throne. A river is where baptism takes place, as is presented in the example of Jesus' baptism in Matthew 3:13.

Let us approach His throne regularly, even daily, so that we can be bathed in His fire and baptized with His Holy Spirit.

Would you consider asking Jesus to baptize you with fire and the Holy Spirit? If this is not something you can do in faith (and whatsoever is not of faith is sin according to Romans 14:23) would you ask Him to begin to give you a desire to be baptized in His fire and an understanding of that. You'll see a desire for Jesus' fire begin to grow in you and you will receive faith and a passion to receive that baptism of fire.

It is when we have been baptized in the fire of God that we become "consuming fire" ourselves and able to be used to bind and loose God's enemy and call down, or apply, the fire of God to the enemy. The more we are immersed in the fire of God the more aflame we ourselves become, just as the longer a piece of firewood stays in the fire, the more thoroughly on fire it becomes.

Let's go to the river for a baptism often...

"There is coming a day when God will judge His enemies little by little, one by one, and consume them with His fire...I believe we are at that day."

Chapter 5

Jesus, the One With Eyes of Fire!

Imagine everything that Jesus looked at becoming set on fire. Imagine looking into His eyes and seeing a flaming fire, and looking until you yourself become ablaze with His fire.

The Word of God says that Jesus' eyes are eyes of fire. We see this in Revelation 1:14, 2:18, and 19:12. This fire is a fire of jealousy, as presented in the Word of God. In Numbers 25:11 the Lord was jealous and considered "consuming" Israel. In Deuteronomy 29:20 the Lord's jealousy "smoked" against His people. Psalm 79:5 says, *"How long, LORD? wilt thou be angry for ever? shall thy jealousy burn like fire?"* Proverbs 6:34 describes jealousy as having "rage," something that fire also possesses. Ezekiel 38:19 ties God's jealousy to the "fire of His wrath." Zephaniah 1:18 and 3:18 both refer to the "fire of God's jealousy."

The fire of God is a fire related to, or incited by, His jealousy.

Why is God a jealous God? Why is Jesus jealous?

Jesus is jealous for His Church, His bride.

Jesus is jealous for His bride, His church. He died to redeem us as His very own, so He could have a bride. Paul caught a glimpse of this jealousy and wrote in II Corinthians 11:2, *"For I am jealous over you with Godly jealousy: for I have espoused you to one husband, that I may present [you as] a chaste virgin to Christ."* Paul was just feeling what God the Father and Jesus feel as described in Scripture. Jesus chose us. He chose to pursue us. This is really represented well in the story of Ruth and Boaz. Boaz didn't have to desire Ruth. He didn't have to want her for his very own and give of himself and his own to redeem her, but he did! He let her have access to his fields, his crops. He then told his servants to make sure they dropped handfuls of grain on purpose so that she could easily get the provision she needed for her and Naomi. Boaz then extended his hand to Ruth and she became his wife, and all that he had became hers. He desired her so he exercised his legal right of redemption to save her.[10]

Jesus desired us. He foresaw us coming to Him, so He laid down His life to redeem us. He then gave us all that He had...all His inheritance from the Father He gave to us. That's why Romans 8:32 says that God, not sparing His own Son for us, will "freely give us all

---

[10] Ruth 2-3 (KJV)

things." And Romans 8:17 says that we are set to inherit jointly all that Jesus has coming to Him.

Jesus died to redeem us, then Jesus exercised His legal right to redeem us. He had made us for Himself as we see in John 1:3. *"All things were made by him; and without him was not any thing made that was made."* I Corinthians 1:16 says, *"For by him were all things created...all things were created by him, and for him..."* He had the right to redeem us.

Jesus is purifying us for Himself, making us a spotless bride. (Ephesians 5:27)

He is jealous for His bride. We cannot imagine the love He has for us. We cannot have that kind of love for each other this side of our glorified state so we cannot understand His passionate love for us. The closest we can come is to compare how we cherish our spouse and would give ourselves, our life, to protect them. And even that example is only as good as our faith walk and our relationship to our spouse.

Jesus loves His bride so much that He laid down His Kingship and all that He had at the Father's side to come and die for us (Philippians 2:6-8). He is jealous for us. He is anxiously awaiting the day that the enemy, who has come to steal our affection, or to harm us, or to divert our attention from the "family" business, will be destroyed. The day is now!!! Jesus has already accomplished this and is waiting for us to avail ourselves of His power and carry out that sentence that has been passed upon the enemy.

Though it will be a process over time, the time for it to begin is here!

He is jealous for us to be baptized in His fire and become His vessels of fire.

Jesus is jealous for His national people Israel.

Jesus is jealous for His national people, Israel, to come to Him. Jesus, in His natural body, is a Jew. God chose, of all the nations of the earth, the bloodline of Abraham, Isaac and Jacob to send His Spirit into a human body and call His name Jesus. He chose to use Jews to put in writing His revelation down through history and give us the written Word of God. He chose the Jews to birth the Living Word of God into flesh and blood. He is jealous for the day their eyes will be opened and the veil of deceit and blindness removed from them (Romans 11:25 and 26).

I think this is hard for us Gentile Christians to understand sometimes. We were raised, whether we like to hear it or not, with a degree of anti-Semitism. It is bread in our Christian culture, not from New Testament Christianity, but from what we've inherited from Constantine, Martin Luther, and many other so called "church fathers" who have influenced what we have known of as the church.

THANK GOD THAT IS CHANGING!

God is opening our eyes to that fact that we, the Gentile church, are just the prerequisite to all Israel being saved. That is so clearly stated in Romans 11:25 and 26.

Jesus, a Jew, longs for His national people to have their eyes opened and see that He is indeed their Yeshua, Messiah. He longs for them to come to the Father so that He can "...forgive them, for they know not what they do." Jesus longs for Israel to ask the question of Him from Zechariah 13:6, "what are those wounds in Your hands," so that He can reply, "those that I received in the house of My friends." Can you just imagine—will you try to—the intense anxiousness Jesus must feel for that time to come, knowing that it will. Anxiousness is probably not the right word, but expectancy is.

Jesus is jealous for all who are or will be His.

God the Father knows, in His foreknowledge, who will come to Him by faith (Romans 8:29). Jesus may well have access to this information in His position as the Son of God, though He gave up the knowledge of some things in His coming to earth (Mark 13:32) Jesus is jealous for those who are going to accept His sacrifice and come to God by faith in Him. He longs to be one with those who are going to be conformed to His image. They are part of His bride. They are part of those promised Him by the Father (John 17:6-22).

Jesus is jealous for them as a man is for his bride he is engaged to. I have some personal experience here.

Jesus is jealous for "...one new man."

Ephesians 2:15 teaches several awesome things, but one of the things we see there is that Jesus died to make Israel and the Gentiles "one new man." Jesus is anxious for Jew and Gentile to worship God through His name and recognize that He is indeed Messiah, so making peace.

As Christian believers in Yeshua we are to, we must, go back to our Jewish roots that we inherited from the early church apostles, prophets and Jesus Himself. They are our foundation principles (Ephesians 2:20-22). These include the feasts of the Lord assigned to us in Leviticus 23 and, more foundational than that, Shabbat or Sabbath. I heard Robert Heidler of Glory of Zion International say recently, speaking about the church, that "Rome is not our mother...Jerusalem is." Amen!

In this process of returning to our Jewish roots which were made illegal by Constantine and left out of our "church life" for centuries, I have heard the Lord caution me to be careful and avoid Jewish traditions that were not Biblical mandates. While we are not to return to some bondage that Jesus died to deliver us from, we are to be walking in the foundational truths of life and success that caused Abraham to prosper, and his descendants after him for the most part. After all, we are of the faith of our father Abraham (Romans 4:12). As we faithfully allow the Holy Spirit of Yeshua Who lives in us, to guide us, He will restore what was robbed from us of our Hebraic roots. In so doing He will use us to bring Israel to jealousy and draw her to Himself, thus bringing about the "one new man" He has promised and that He so longs for.

I heard someone teaching on this "one new man" concept and he stated that when God brings us to the place of "one new man" it will produce a creature or being (man) that has never existed before. I personally believe that, and I believe the enemy is terrified of the resulting person that God will form in the "new man". This is because it will be a believer so filled with Jesus and all that God intended from Adam through Abraham, Moses, David and Christ Himself, that it will bring about the destroying of the enemy.

Jesus is jealous to see this one new man. He sits "expectantly" on His throne awaiting His enemies to be made to bow at His feet and be put under His feet. There is a fire in His eyes that burns with longing and passion to see this come about!

Jesus is waiting to impart to use that very fire and the knowledge of how to use it as He would!

Do not fear the fire in Jesus' eyes. It is fueled and fanned by His jealousy for you and me to be all <u>He</u> has destined us for.

"There is coming a day when God will judge His enemies little by little, one by one, and consume them with His fire...I believe we are at that day."

Chapter 6

God's Fire—a Purifying Fire

What is the place that we most quickly think of as the place of fire? Hell. And it was not made for people (though many people will spend eternity there), but for the devil and his angels (Matthew 25:41).

However, God does have a fire that is meant for His people, a fire that does a work in His people—a purifying work.

Malachi 3:1-4 teaches that God will send His messenger to prepare the way before Him and that this messenger will serve as a refiner of gold and silver. He will be a purifying messenger to purify as with soap and fire. His purpose will be to make ready the Levites to offer sacrifices in righteousness in God's temple. I think this is so important that I feel I should include the quote:

"Behold, I will send my messenger, and he shall prepare the way before me: and the Lord, whom ye seek, shall suddenly come to his temple, even the messenger of the covenant, whom ye delight in: behold, he shall come, saith the LORD of hosts. But who may abide the day of his coming? and who shall stand when he appeareth? for he is like a refiner's

fire, and like fullers' soap: And he shall sit as a refiner and purifier of silver: and he shall purify the sons of Levi, and purge them as gold and silver, that they may offer unto the LORD an offering in righteousness. Then shall the offering of Judah and Jerusalem be pleasant unto the LORD, as in the days of old, and as in former years." Malachi 3:1-4 (KJV)

Jesus is presented here as God's messenger, "the Lord Whom we seek," to serve as a refiner's fire.

Obviously, Jesus is the ultimate refiner of gold and silver, but I believe any of us can be used of God to fulfill this role. After all, we are to walk in the example of Christ in life and ministry.

This book is given to the fact that we are to become God's vessels of fire, devouring the enemy as we are enveloped in God's fire.

Jesus actually gave Himself to that end. We've talked about the fact that Jesus was/is a baptizer in fire. Jesus stated that He came to send or scatter fire on the earth. This is strange! My dad reminded me of this two days before this writing as we were discussing parts of this book. I had forgotten that the Word of God states such...I had so forgotten it that it was like I was learning new truth when I looked up the passage. In Luke 12:49 and 50 Jesus said that He had come to send fire on the earth and that the fire was already kindled. The word "send" is a sowing word meaning to "scatter as in sowing seed." This same passage seems to teach that Jesus was to be baptized Himself with fire. The passage reads:

"I am come to send fire on the earth; and what will I, if it be already kindled? But I have a baptism to be baptized with; and how am I straitened till it be accomplished!" Jesus was both baptized with fire and He was to baptize us with fire (Matthew 3:11, 12; Luke 3:16.17). In these Scriptures we see Jesus baptizing us with fire and having a "fan in His hand." This fan was for threshing, the process of removing the chaff from the wheat.

Jesus, the Refiner sent from Father to go before Him and prepare the way, is fanning us to separate the chaff from the valued, life filled wheat. He is doing this to make us readied, life-bearing vessels that can fill the role and purpose God has for us in His Kingdom.

As we will see in the entirety of this book, Jesus is also going to make us refiners, burning embers of His fire, so that we are devouring agents of His enemy as we move about the Kingdom and take dominion for Him.

Paul caught a glimpse of this. That's why He wrote in I Corinthians 3:12 that everyone who builds upon Jesus' foundation is going to have their work tried. It's unavoidable...when you build something on a fire, what you erect is tried by that fire. All that remains will be "gold, silver and precious stones", that which is usable in God's Kingdom.

This is all a part of the role of the refiner and the purpose of the refiner's fire. You can see that as you study all that the Word of God has to say about gold, silver and precious stones. Just compare Malachi 3:1-4 with I Chronicles 29:1-9, and then I Corinthians 3:12. God's fire consumes all that is not of Him and makes all that is more pure, stronger, more beautiful, and of more value for use in His temple and for His Kingdom purposes.

Thank God for His fire that is purifying us even now. Would you ask Holy Spirit to prepare you to go to a new place of refining. Jesus was baptized with fire then scattered or sowed fire in the earth. Now He is to baptize us with fire so we can be the ones sowing His fire in the earth. Ask Him to prepare you for a new and deeper visitation of Jesus, God's refining fire...

> *"There is coming a day when God will judge His enemies little by little, one by one, and consume them with His fire...I believe we are at that day."*

Chapter 7

Step Boldly Into the River of Fire!!!

Come boldly to the throne of grace...that's what we are commanded to do by God. That's how we are commanded to come to His throne, the throne of grace. Hebrews 4:16 says, *"Let us therefore come boldly unto the throne of grace, that we may obtain mercy, and find grace to help in time of need."* When God extends this opportunity to us it is an invitation to step into His presence, or bow in His presence. However, if we analyze this opportunity God is really *commanding us to step into His river of fire.*

God did not simply invite us to come boldly to His throne. He actually commands it. Hebrews chapter 4 is a very severe and serious chapter. Check out verses 1 and 11. *"Let us therefore fear, lest, a promise being left us of entering into his rest, any of you should seem to come short of it... Let us labour therefore to enter into that rest, lest any man fall after the same example of unbelief."* For that matter, read the whole chapter. It builds upon itself. Verse 16 is a command to approach God's throne...to come boldly to the throne of grace so that we can receive mercy and grace to help in time of need.

God's throne is the mercy seat where the fiery presence of God comes down. This is seen somewhat clearly if we read carefully Hebrews 8, 9 and 10. According to Romans 12[11] our bodies are living sacrifices, so when we approach the throne of God we become the living sacrifice placed upon the mercy seat that the fire of God falls upon to consume. However, when God's fire consumes something that has been offered to Him, He simply refines that part of the offering that is eternal. He only burns up that which is temporary. This is the picture and understanding we get from I Corinthians 3:12-14.

In Daniel 7:9 and 10 we see that God's throne is seated in fire and issues forth fire. *"I beheld till the thrones were cast down, and the Ancient of days did sit, whose garment was white as snow, and the hair of his head like the pure wool: his throne was like the fiery flame, and his wheels as burning fire. A fiery stream issued and came forth from before him: thousand thousands ministered unto him, and ten thousand times ten thousand stood before him: the judgment was set, and the books were opened."* Some translations clearly state that "a river" of fire flowed from God's throne. Young's Literal Translation says that a "flood of fire" proceeded from the throne of God. So when we are urged or commanded to come boldly to the throne of grace we are being commanded to step into God's river of fire. Wow! This puts new meaning into "coming boldly" before His throne of grace.

---

[11] Romans 12:! (KJV)

Though most of us do not realize it, all who seek God's presence are seeking His fire. I have been amazed in studying for this book, just following the leads Holy Spirit gives, how much there is in the Word of God about the fire of God. Beginning in 2007 when God began to teach me the prayer and warfare strategy represented in this book, He began to show me that His fire is something that we should come to not be afraid of. *We should let Him remove our fear of the fire of God.* God's fire is only destructive to all that opposes Him and His purposes. His fire only purifies that which is of Him, that which is eternal.

God's whole throne environment is fire. His throne is as a fiery flame. His throne has wheels that are fire (Daniel 7:9). And, there is the river of fire flowing from His throne. As we obey God and come into His throne room presence we are *engaged in His fire* and all about us that is not of Him is consumed, little by little, more and more with each appearance at His throne, from glory unto glory. This has the effect of making us a "consuming fire" just as our God and His Christ are, so that He can use us to bind and loose the enemy and call down the fire of God to destroy it, and by so doing claim our cities for His Kingdom purposes.

<u>So COME ON...step boldly into the river of fire!</u>

> *"There is coming a day when God will judge His enemies little by little, one by one, and consume them with His fire...I believe we are at that day."*

Chapter 8

Preparing the Way for God's Advance

Did you ever wonder why God's throne has wheels? I didn't even know that it did until fairly recently. Chances are you did not either. Daniel 7:9 indicates that God's throne sits on wheels. It says, *"I beheld till the thrones were cast down, and the Ancient of days did sit, whose garment [was] white as snow, and the hair of his head like the pure wool: his throne [was like] the fiery flame, [and] his wheels [as] burning fire."* The NKJV says it this way: *"I watched till thrones were put in place, And the Ancient of Days was seated; His garment was white as snow, And the hair of His head was like pure wool. His throne was a fiery flame, Its wheels a burning fire."* (NKJV ™) I questioned the Lord about this recently and this is what He showed me, as I have entered into my journal:

> *"In Psalm 97:3 we find that a fire goes before God and burns up all His enemies. This fire, I believe, is in a swirling motion around God's throne. This is born out in the fact that Psalm 97:3 says the fire burns up all His enemies round about Him. The Hebrew word for this is the same used*

of the winds making their circuits from south to north in continuous motion.

As I was meditating on this verse I kind of questioned the Lord about this and He gave me this further insight. God's throne is on wheels of fire. We see this in Daniel 7:9. When God reminded me of this and I asked Him about it, He showed me that this is for the advancement of His Kingdom. His Kingdom is on the move, conquering and retaking territory that He created for His purposes. So, His throne, the place where He sits in authority in His Kingdom, has wheels, wheels of advancement. These wheels are of fire because nothing can be before Him in His presence that is not purified. All things are tried and purified by fire (I Corinthians 3:12-14). So, not only do we step into God's fire and become purified when we come boldly to the throne of grace, as He has urged us to do, but as His Kingdom advances the wheels His throne moves on are a burning fire consuming everything that opposes Him before He sees it. When He chooses to advance into a new territory His fire begins to prepare the way for His authority. This is why the enemy hates the sound of the shofar blown by God's people in the season it is to be blown (new moons, feasts of the Lord, beginnings of gatherings of God's people, etc...). Because the shofar announces God's intent to move into a territory and stake it as His own, when the enemy hears the shofar He knows God's fire is on the way to consume. God's wheels of fire are advancing the enemy's way and he will now be consumed."

Psalm 97:3 says a fire goes before God. The Hebrew word for "goes before Him" is "paniym". Strong's Concordance defines this word as "the part of the face that turns". It is used to call us to seek His face, His presence. For example, in Psalm 100 we are told that we are to come before His presence ("paniym") with singing and in Psalm 95:2 with thanksgiving. What we are being told here is that our approaching God with singing and thanksgiving causes Him to turn His face to us. Wow! This also means that God won't even turn His face to anything that has not been first tested in His fire to see what sort it is. He tells us that He is too holy to look upon sin (Habakkuk 1:13: *"Thou art of purer eyes than to behold evil, and canst not look on iniquity..."*) So God has His fire precede His face before it turns, to consume all that He chooses not to look upon, all that is unholy. This should really encourage us...He has, through Jesus, made us approachable to Him and His eye is upon us. He even promises to guide us with His eye.

God is holy and will not tolerate sin in His presence. In other words, that which "misses the mark" (the definition of "sin") of God's perfection will not be allowed in His presence. So, He sends fire before Himself to devour all that is unholy and to purify and refine His possession. Jesus is the ultimate refiner. Malachi 3:1-4 is talking specifically about Jesus in His role as purifier.

> *"Behold, I will send my messenger, and he shall prepare the way before me:*

and the Lord, whom ye seek, shall suddenly come to his temple, even the messenger of the covenant, whom ye delight in: behold, he shall come, saith the LORD of hosts. But who may abide the day of his coming? and who shall stand when he appeareth? for he is like a refiner's fire, and like fullers' soap: And he shall sit as a refiner and purifier of silver: and he shall purify the sons of Levi, and purge them as gold and silver, that they may offer unto the LORD an offering in righteousness. Then shall the offering of Judah and Jerusalem be pleasant unto the LORD, as in the days of old, and as in former years."

So, we see that Jesus is the purifier, the refiner's fire. However, the entire Word of God emphasizes that Jesus is ordaining us to be His instruments to spread His Kingdom and to conquer territory for His purposes. Psalm 115:16 tells us that God has given the earth to man...this is our domain. Psalm 8:1-6 teaches that God made man to have dominion in the earth, simply repeating the creation theme of Genesis 1:28. We are to be "followers of Christ" with Him as our example. Jesus is a refiner and purifier going before and preparing the way for God's habitation. If this were a Biblical Psalm this would be a good place for a "Selah"—so take a minute and think on this. You and I are to be as Jesus, a refiner's fire so that we prepare the way for the advance of God's presence in and through us. Fire prepares the way for God's advance. We, too, are to become God's firebrands, purifying territory and consuming the enemy. What a privilege you and I have—to be given the role and opportunity to purify the place that God will occupy— or at least to go before Him asking for His fiery presence to purify the place we want Him to inhabit.

"There is coming a day when God will judge His enemies little by little, one by one, and consume them with His fire...I believe we are at that day."

Chapter 9

God—a Wall of Fire About You

The history of the fire of God has not always been friendly to humanity. There are quite a few instances in the Bible where people were destroyed by it. That is not God's intent for His people. Really, it's not His intent for any person. He even says that hell was not made for man but for the devil and his angels, or demons.

God's intent for us is to be surrounded with his fire so that we are purified, filled with His glory, and have a protective wall of fire around us that the enemy cannot penetrate—then we are vessels of His fire. We can then take the fire to places and things that need to be purified and to those of His enemy whose time it is to be destroyed. Any believer in Jesus is destined for this. This is part of our being predestined to be conformed to the image of God's Son, Jesus.[12]

I remember the old song from my childhood that talks about this. It's funny...it had been so long since I had sang the song in church I had forgotten the title so I googled it. It is "Lily of the Valley", and the funny thing is, George Jones has recorded it on a gospel album.

---

[12] Romans 8:28-31 (KJV)

That's not really the source I had expected to find when I searched for the lyrics. One verse of this song says that God is "...a wall of fire about me, I've nothing now to fear. With His manna He my hungry soul shall fill."

This is Bible doctrine. These lyrics come from Zechariah 2:5 which says:

> *"For I, saith the LORD, will be unto her a wall of fire round about, and will be the glory in the midst of her."*

First of all, this is talking about the city of Jerusalem. So why shouldn't we dismiss this verse as not being about us individually. Why should we think this is for our family or our business or congregation, for us as intercessors and warriors? The first reason is because all the Word of God has individual application.

Second, the Word of God is prophecy and the nature of the prophetic is that anyone who accepts it receives of its life. That's why when I hear Mary's response to the Holy Spirit telling her that she was going to conceive seed from God Himself, "...be it unto Thy servant as Thou hast said," and I receive that as the Word of God to me, Jesus' life is born in me. This means that I receive his eternal life and I receive His creative ideas and witty inventions to produce life giving things here on earth.

The third and main reason that we can know this wall of fire is for us is because we are individual stones that make up the New Jerusalem. Revelation 21:2 says, *"And I John saw the holy city, new Jerusalem, coming down from God out of heaven, prepared as a bride adorned for her husband."* The New Jerusalem is the bride. This is plainly stated in Revelation 21:9 & 10. Each of us as believers and members of the body of Christ are a stone in the eternal temple God is building. *"And I heard a great voice out of heaven saying, Behold, the tabernacle of God is with men, and he will dwell with them..."* This is from Revelation 21:3. I Peter 2:5 teaches us that we are living stones in a spiritual house God is building. Ephesians 2:19-22 teaches that each of us as individual saints is built into a temple of the Lord. From these 3 passages we see that the bride of Christ is the New Jerusalem, and that each of us are a stone in the temple of God, the New Jerusalem and God's eternal habitation.

So God can be a wall of fire about us!

Now that we have that out of the way, what does this wall of fire really mean to us?

This wall is a protective wall of fire. In Zechariah 2:1-5 we see in the context that Jerusalem is going to be so vastly inhabited that it cannot have walls...the population will expand beyond the walls. Walls cannot contain it. So God will be her wall of protection with His fire surrounding Jerusalem.

His fire will be so all consuming of the enemy, darkness, and sin that His glory will be within

Jerusalem and within His wall of fire. God's "kabod", His weighty presence, will invade the city because His fire is so intense as it surrounds Jerusalem that it consumes all evil and makes way for the presence of God. Again, Zechariah 2:5 says, *"For I, saith the LORD, will be unto her a wall of fire round about, and will be the glory in the midst of her."*

The next thing, and the most applicable to this book, is that God's intense wall of fire will consume the enemy as it would approach God's people. I was visiting with a friend in one of the Grenadine Islands recently and he relayed the following story:

> He said that someone involved in some form of witchcraft was present in one of their church services on the island one day, sent by the group he was a part of, to try to infiltrate their congregation. When my friend became aware of who he was he went to him and told him to return to his group and tell them not to send him again or God's fire would destroy him. At that, the man drew up and contorted as if to withdraw himself from the mention of the fire of God.

Make no mistake, the demons know about the fire of God. They know that Jesus is the Refiner with a fire that will consume them and their purposes, and their demented master. This man was simply reacting to the demonic presence in him and giving us a demonstration of how the fire of God will be a protective wall of fire about us.

God's wall of fire around His people will form an intense wall of destruction to consume the enemy as he would approach. I wonder how many times we've been spared by this wall of fire and didn't know it, because it is a fire invisible to the human eye.

This wall of fire will become increasingly more important to us as we gain greater responsibility in God's army and as the body of Christ comes nearer and nearer completely taking the Kingdom of God violently and by force (Matthew 11:12). It is necessary for us to exercise our authority to bind, and loose, and call down the fire of God on His enemy.

Would you right now ask God to thicken and intensify His wall of fire that is surrounding you as a member of the body of Christ and as one of His intercessors and warriors?

"There is coming a day when God will judge His enemies little by little, one by one, and consume them with His fire...I believe we are at that day."

Chapter 10

Catch Fire With His fire!

Jesus said that He had come to scatter fire in the earth!

This is a very strong statement when you think about it. It is found in Luke 12:49 & 50 which say, *"I am come to send fire on the earth; and what will I, if it be already kindled? But I have a baptism to be baptized with; and how am I straitened till it be accomplished!"* When Jesus says that He came to "send" fire on the earth, the Greek word used is "ballo". It means to "scatter, throw or cast into". Another meaning is "to throw or let go of a thing without caring where it falls." This reminds me of a dream I heard a preacher and apostolic leader share. He said he had dreamed he saw Jesus riding across the United States of America on a horse casting fire to the ground in certain places, almost at random if, I remember correctly the way he shared the dream. He said that in the dream wherever Jesus' fire fell the power of God broke out on those regions and awesome things began to happen with people coming to Jesus in mass and miracles taking place. This dream accurately matches the part of Jesus' assignment presented in Luke 12:49.

He scatters fire by scattering His Word which possesses the fire of God. He scatters fire by visitations of Himself in the earth realm. He scatters fire by simply looking with His eyes of fire on a region. He also scatters His fire by making you and me, His ministers, a flaming fire and sending us into the earth to scatter His fire. Jesus scatters fire in the earth through His people, setting us on fireby baptizing us in God's river of fire. Maybe it was His people He was using to scatter fire in the dream mentioned above. This is multiplication according to Heaven's method of multiplying. That's why Jesus could say, "greater works than these" we would do...He was referring to His body of believers.

God is drawing us to His river of fire.

> There is a river, whose streams make glad the city of God (Psalm 46:4).

> God *"showed me a pure river of water of life, clear as crystal, proceeding out of the throne of God"* (Revelation 22:1).

> Jesus said, *"He that believes on me out of his belly shall flow rivers of living water..."* (John 7:38)

These are all passages in God's Word that He uses to intrigue us and draw us to His river.

Man is naturally intrigued by rivers. That's why waterfront property is of such premium value. If we studied the origin of this we'd find that its roots go back to the first people to settle any land. Water is necessary for life...it is the water of life. So naturally, people wanted to settle on land accessible to water. Water is also beautiful to look at. I think even this is probably tied to the fact that water is so life giving and such a carrier of life to all flesh. We are drawn to what gives us life.

God draws us to His river.

God's river is a river of life, and it is also a river of fire. John saw the river of water flowing from God's throne and wrote about it in Revelation 22:1. Daniel saw the river as a river of fire and made a journal of it for us (Daniel 7:9).

I believe they were seeing the same river with two elements...both cleansing elements and both elements that God has and will use to judge.

Now let's consider this river of fire.

As we step into God's river of fire we become firebrands ourselves. We become burning embers, but much more than just embers...firebrands or torches! Jesus baptizes us in His river. The law or rule of first mention in Bible study applies here. Baptism is first mentioned as happening in a river (John 3:6). Jesus was baptized in a river. Jesus baptized in a river (John 3:22, 23). Jesus still baptizes in a river— God's river of fire. When we approach God's throne we step into His river of fire. We must, because it precedes His throne and issues out of it. There is no other way to access God's throne except through the river of fire.

Now let's take that a step further. Another really great thing about this thought is that when two or more catch fire the fire intensifies. One can chase a thousand but two can put ten thousand to flight. When we get more burning embers we have a hotter, bigger, more intense fire. Proverbs 26:20 & 21 talks about this. It says that where no wood is the fire goes out and likewise where no murmurer is the strife ceases. As coals are to burning coals, and wood to fire, so is a contentious person to kindle strife. God demonstrated this to me a few days before this writing—I was on my way to the doctor to try to get relief from a terribly painful illness I had gotten. I had prayed against this disease and warred against it using the prayer strategy in this book but found little relief. Before I left for the doctor's office my wife laid her hands on me and prayed and accessed the fire of God against the enemy on my behalf. As I drove to my appointment I realized that God had answered my wife's prayer and that I had great relief from pain. I asked the Father why my prayer hadn't been effective. Was this such a powerful demon that my faith wasn't strong enough to deal with it, even using such an effective prayer strategy? The Lord's response to me was that when Denie prayed with me we joined forces and "two put ten thousand to flight." She simply added her faith and prayer to my already existing faith and prayer and together we saw a victory I hadn't been able to see by myself.

I know we can't see God's fire with our natural eyes, but neither can we see God's throne with our natural eyes. We accept God's throne and it is a part of our faith. This river of fire must become a part of our faith —our belief system—especially to those of us who are intercessors and warriors and to those who intend to take Kingdom territory for God and see Jesus become Lord of their city and region.

As we spend time at God's throne Jesus baptizes us in this river of fire.

Let us not be like Peter was initially. When Jesus began to wash His feet he said, "You're my Lord. You'll never wash my feet." Then Jesus explained it to him. After that Peter said, "...not my feet only but also my hands and my head..." Wash all of me, Lord! (John 13:5-9)

We must spend enough time at God's throne for Jesus to baptize us in this river and for the fire to consume all of us that is not eternal, and to purify what's left of us that is eternal.

This fire is a necessary element of our Kingdom work in this hour in which we live.

As we step into His river of fire we become flaming torches for His purposes. "He makes...His ministers a flaming fire." (Hebrews 1:7)

His fire will ultimately consume all His enemies, all wickedness from the earth. Psalm 104:35 teaches this when it says, *"...let the sinners be consumed out of the earth, and let the wicked be no more. Bless thou the LORD, O my soul. Praise ye the LORD."* I Corinthians 15:26 teaches us that all God's enemies will be destroyed and death will be destroyed last. We know from John's writing in Revelation 20:14 that death will be destroyed by fire. A careful study of Scripture reveals that God's instrument of destruction for His enemies is fire. We are carriers of this fire, and we are His servants to carry out the consuming of God's enemies, those being Satan and his demonic spirits. We will see this more clearly as we complete this book...

It is imperative that we catch fire with His fire! Jesus desires to baptize us in His fire. Let us approach God's throne of grace daily so that we can wade into His river of fire and receive Jesus' baptism.

Let Him set us on fire so that WE become His consuming fire!

"There is coming a day when God will judge His enemies little by little, one by one, and consume them with His fire...I believe we are at that day."

Chapter 11

Judge Nothing Before it's Time

This is a very important chapter in this book—it may be the most important. I almost placed this chapter before the chapter detailing the prayer strategy that is the focus of this book, chapter two. It is so important that you and I understand and submit to God's timing in everything, or see failure. Please read carefully and understand this chapter before moving too deeply into the prayer strategy given in chapter two.

God is excited about judging His enemies. He is excited about the day that they all will be consumed from the earth, so it can be a place used to accomplish His creative purposes without those being hindered. God is excited about earth being a place of His complete shalom, the environment of His throne. So why doesn't He just go ahead and consume the enemy now? Why is it in stages that God consumes the enemy? And it is, as is indicated in I Corinthians 15:26, which says, *"The last enemy that shall be destroyed ..."*

There are reasons that God will destroy His enemy in stages. What is ESSENTIAL is that we cooperate with Him and walk in His timing as we partner with Him in becoming vessels of fire to consume the enemy.

God gives ample example in the Bible of this idea. In Genesis 15:14-16 we see God holding off judgment on the Amorites because their iniquity was not yet *"full"*. Once this fullness happened God moved, the enemy withholding His promise in Abraham was removed, and God completed what He had promised 400 years before.

God has created both the evil and the good. Proverbs 16:4 says that the Lord has made even the wicked for the day of evil. He demonstrated this in Pharaoh. He told Pharaoh that He had raised him up to show in him His power (Romans 9:17). God didn't destroy Pharaoh; he set him in position to feed His very small nation of Israel—through Joseph— when it was only Jacob, his sons and their families. Then, 400 years later, God used Pharaoh to test His people by opposing them. He then used him as an example of His salvation of His people as He destroyed Pharaoh and his army.

Later in the wilderness, after Israel crossed the Red Sea, God chose to destroy their enemies one by one and not all at once. This is so powerful that I want to enter the Scripture here so we can see it:

> *"I will send my fear before thee, and will destroy all the people to whom thou shalt come, and I will make all thine enemies turn their backs unto thee. And I will send hornets before thee, which shall drive out the Hivite, the Canaanite, and the Hittite, from before*

thee. I will not drive them out from before thee in one year; lest the land become desolate, and the beast of the field multiply against thee. By little and little I will drive them out from before thee, until thou be increased, and inherit the land. And I will set thy bounds from the Red sea even unto the sea of the Philistines, and from the desert unto the river: for I will deliver the inhabitants of the land into your hand; and thou shalt drive them out before thee." (Exodus 23:27-31)

Notice a couple of things in the above Scripture. *God saw ALL Israel's enemies destroyed before any of them were.* We must let Him increase our faith so that we see our enemies, His enemies, like He does.

Also, we see that He refused, in His wisdom, to destroy the enemies all at once. He was going to take what to us would seem like a long time...He would take over a year to destroy these enemies. This was relatively a long time to Israel who was on what should have been a fairly short trip, had they not extended it to 40 years by their fear, unbelief and rebellion. But to God, this year was not long...God had a purpose and He wanted <u>all</u> His purpose to be fulfilled.

Another demonstration of this occurs with Jesus. In Matthew 8:29 we find Him encountering demons in two men. When they met Jesus they cried out, "...are you come to torment us before our time..." It's as if even the devils know their fate is sealed and their destruction certain. They are bent on their way of evil and to destruction because they chose to follow Satan and set their destiny. They cannot stop their evil and their fighting against God though they know that their very actions are increasing the wrath that will ultimately be poured out on them. They were aware that there was some future time set for their destruction, but not that time.

God's set time for the total and final judgment of His enemy will last a long time according to our way of measuring time. It's my opinion from Scripture that it will last 1000 years. But with God it will be at just the right time and span and will be done in the way that will most glorify and please Him, and fulfill His purpose. I believe that time has arrived, or is within sight, and God is preparing His people for their shared role in it.

Had God destroyed Satan before Jesus came, He could not have used him to usher in His plan of redemption through Jesus' blood and salvation through His resurrection.

God still has a time table for the destruction of the enemy. We have to let Him work in us in this regard. We have to wait on Him and move in His time table. This time table is established, and must be walked out in us by faith. THIS IS HUGE! We must discern and walk in God's time to enforce His Kingdom.

We are judges ourselves.

I want to address for a moment the fact that <u>we</u> are taking part in this "judgment" on God's enemy.

Our mindset is that God is the judge, and He is. We find that plainly stated in Psalm 50:6 which says, *"...God is judge Himself."* Psalm 75:7 and Acts 10:42 also teach this, among other Scripture.

However, we see over and over in Scripture passages like Psalm 115:16 where God tells us that the heavens are His but He has given the earth to man. The word "given" is the Hebrew word "nathan". It means to give, bestow, deliver to, and to <u>entrust</u>. God has entrusted to us the keeping of the earth He has made for us. This includes the government of man. This includes all we allow in our sphere here on earth. He has given us the authority to order it after His heart and make decisions, judgment, as to its use and care.

Revelation 6:10 is a description of God's saints crying out at His throne for His judgment and avenging of the blood they shed for His Kingdom. I Corinthians 6:2 & 3 presents us as judges, both of the "things of this world" and of angels, and demons are just fallen angels.

In Psalm 5:2 is a very interesting teaching. I'll paraphrase what is says..."unto You will I pray, Lord. My voice You will hear in the morning. In the morning I will direct my prayer unto You and will look up...for You are not a God that has pleasure in wickedness, neither shall evil dwell with You." If you study the Hebrew text you will find that a very literal translation of this is, "Hear my judgment and intercession for that judgment to begin...in the morning I will set in order or set the battle in array and will keep my watch. For You are not a God that has pleasure in wickedness, neither shall evil dwell with you..." Here we see David crying out to God after having made judgment on a situation and now interceding for that judgment to take place. He is also setting the battle in array as he stands his morning watch. He is keeping guard of his sphere of the earth, passing judgment and interceding at God's throne for that judgment to take place. This carries with it the idea of decree—man decreeing the judgment that God has ordained on a structure.

Psalm 110 describes a scenario in which Jesus is conquering and ruling in the midst of His enemies with us as His willing agents.

In Daniel 7 we see the Ancient of Days being seated before His tens of thousands of worshipping saints and the scene is described as, "...the judgment was set..." (vs. 10). Verse 26 says, "...But the judgment shall sit and they (I believe the saints) shall take his (the enemy's) dominion..." Revelation 20 and verse 4 gives an amazing insight into the judgment coming from God's throne room area. In what seems to be a scene in which the saints of God are being referenced it says, *"And I saw thrones, and they sat upon them, and judgment was given unto them: and I saw the souls of them that were beheaded for the witness of Jesus, and for the word of God, and which had not worshipped the beast, neither his image, neither had received his mark upon their foreheads, or in their hands; and they lived and reigned with Christ a thousand years."*

All these above passages leave little room to doubt that we have at least a shared, interactive role in God's judgment of the enemy. I believe it is a much stronger role in that God is waiting on us to receive by faith what He's already decreed, agree with it and speak it into action, <u>in His timing</u>. Then He will begin to enact judgment.

We must walk in patient faith!

Without faith it is impossible to please God (Hebrews 11:6). One of the most important things to learn about the prayer strategy in this book, or any for that matter, is that it MUST operate in faith.

About 9 years ago I had an experience related to this subject. I began to pray for the deliverance of a certain pop singer. As I did I thought I heard Holy Spirit say to me, "you don't have the faith to take on the demons around her life..." I immediately backed off. I began a process of learning that God's timing is so critical in deliverance, in binding and/or loosing the enemy, in judging evil. I began learning and walking in the prayer strategy presented in chapter 2 of this book in February of 2007.

One of the chief things I've learned is that *if* I do not have the faith to exercise Jesus' authority over specific spirits in a given situation or place, it will do no good to try, and it could do harm. It could open the door for great harm to me or those in my sphere. That which is not of faith is sin (Romans 14:23). Sin is defined as "missing the mark." We cannot afford to miss the mark in judging the enemy. However, when God gives the faith we move and we exercise Jesus' authority in a circumstance and in a realm.

We have a safeguard.

There is a safeguard in all of this, so that we do not walk into a dangerous situation unawares. God must show us what we are warring against and God must give the faith to remove it.

Discernment is a gift that operates by faith. God does not give faith for discernment before it is time. When He gives this discernment He is either ready to destroy the darkness He has just revealed and identified or He is ready to prepare us for their destruction. At the very least He is making us ready to deal with this evil and remove it, even if its destruction is for a later time. He does not give discernment before its time. Faith is a gift of God (Ephesians 2:8) and He does not give faith out of time.

Have discerning judgment.

We are talking about judgment here. We are talking about God, through His people, judging His enemies. I Corinthians 6:3 says, *"Know ye not that we shall judge angels?"* Demons are fallen angels. Discernment is a New Testament word which means "to judge". In fact, "judge" and "discern" come from the same root Greek word in the New Testament. So it could be said that the gift of discernment is a gift given for the purpose of judgment...they are the same thing.

We are going to judge demons! And we are coming into that season! But, we have to judge them one by one and in God's timing. This is not to say that God will not ever judge His enemies in mass. He has most likely done that in the past. But there is a definite pattern of His judging them one by one in Scripture. We are dealing with occult networks, hidden networks of darkness. They must be uncovered in layers or as a network. They have a hierarchy and must be dealt with in their order.

God really caught my attention with this recently when He said to me, "...Judge nothing before it's time!" I said, "Wow!" Or was it "Whoa!" Actually I said both. I got the concordance and looked that verse up. It is I Corinthians 4:5. I want to quote it because it gives such light on what I've been discussing here. *"Therefore judge nothing before the time, until the Lord come, who both will bring to light the hidden things of darkness, and will make manifest the counsels of the hearts: and then shall every man have praise of God."* This is exactly what I was saying when I said that God won't give discernment on a thing until He's ready for us to deal with it. God began to show me principalities in our region in 2006 so that He could begin to prepare His people in the region to deal with them. This is still in process. I know there are others in our region to whom He is showing these and other things. He is preparing His people for judgment, of His enemies. He is doing this globally. We must be prepared because we cannot judge anything before it's time. Ephesians 5:13 says, *"But all things that are reproved are made manifest by the light: for whatsoever doth make manifest is light."* The word "reprove" means to "expose". The word "manifest" means to make visible and known that which has been unknown. This is the "occult"...that which is hidden. I John 3:8 tells us that Jesus was "manifested" to "destroy the works of the devil."

God must show us what we are warring against with His light, and God must give the faith to remove it. This is part of the role His fire plays in our warfare. Fire is light. It reveals or makes manifest.

God moves in mercy.

There is another last reason that God waits to destroy. He is merciful and wants to give flesh every chance to repent before He destroys it. Thank God for His mercy. Jeremiah wrote in Lamentations 3:22 *"...it is of the Lord's mercies that we are not consumed, because His compassions fail not."*

Flesh is enmity against God. We see this principle in Romans 8:4-8 and in James 4:1-4. This means that unredeemed flesh and flesh that is not Spirit filled is the enemy of God. Psalm 104:35 says. *"Let the sinners be consumed out of the earth, and let the wicked be no more. Bless thou the LORD, O my soul. Praise ye the LORD."* God knows that the day will come when, in His destruction of His adversary, Satan, those who have been willingly deceived by him will also be destroyed. This was made real to me in 2007 and 2008 when God was showing me a major stronghold in our region, probably a principality. During that process I met families in our city whose young children were involved in ball teams and scout troops, etc...that met on the grounds owned and operated by those who were being used as vessels to facilitate and house this stronghold. I realized how entrenched wickedness can be when it has deceived a region for years. God is merciful and He will patiently wait on these innocents who are entrapped in the web of darkness to be set free. We must allow Him to orchestrate the timetable of the dismantling and destruction of the enemy.

Zephaniah 3:8 says:

> *"Therefore <u>wait ye upon me, saith the LORD</u>, until the day that I rise up to the prey: for my determination is to gather the nations, that I may assemble the kingdoms, to pour upon them mine indignation, even all my fierce anger: for all the earth shall be devoured with the fire of my jealousy."*

God has a time set...let us "wait upon Him." Let us allow the Lord to guide us in His wisdom and timeframe so that we "judge nothing before its time." In this we have a safeguard for ourselves, those we love, and those we minister to and minister with. In this God is glorified because we have moved in His timing and walked in His faith.

Jesus is seated far above all principality and power and sees their positioning and maneuvering. This also means that He sees the timing for the destruction of that which is darkness.

We are ordained to be vessels of His judgment. Let us judge nothing before its time. With this mindset as our safeguard, we will not be harmed as we bind, and loose, and call down the fire of God on His enemies.

"There is coming a day when God will judge His enemies little by little, one by one, and consume them with His fire...I believe we are at that day."

Chapter 12

Personal Deliverance, Purging and Restoration

I was at Glory of Zion in Denton, Texas during the Rosh Hashana celebration in September of 2009. In one of the sessions the Holy Spirit visited me and I realized that I needed to include a chapter in this book on personal deliverance.

We must have the authority to operate in the spirit realm before we begin to take action. We must have the level of faith necessary to engage a particular demonic spirit before we do so. God has given us that authority in several areas naturally. In other areas we must gain the authority through the proper channels or protocol.

God has given us the authority we need in our sphere of operation. That sphere includes our home as the head of the home, in our business if we are the owner or operator, and by all means in our own body. So, whenever God shows us a strongman in our own lives we are the authority in control to get rid of it. We need only let our faith grow to the level necessary to get rid of it.

It is when enough of us in a region have begun to do this that God gives victory in that territory.

I was meditating in Psalm 119 early one morning. When I got to verse 84 Holy Spirit quickened me. I was under some personal warfare that morning and began to retaliate with the fire of God, as I describe in this book. The Lord began to show me that this was a very key verse for this chapter on personal deliverance, purging, victory and laying aside every weight and the sin that so easily would beset us.

Psalm 119:84 asks the question, *"How many are the days of Your servant? When will You execute judgment on those who persecute me?"* As I read this verse I realized that when the psalmist asked this, even then God was waiting on His people to come to the place where they could engage the enemy with the warfare that would dismantle and destroy him. This particular section of Psalm 119, the 11th section, starts with verse 81. It addresses God and says *"...My soul faints for Your salvation..."* I can almost hear God's reply to us now when we read that verse, now that Jesus has come, died, risen and conquered the greatest enemy of all. He must wonder why we are not availing ourselves of His power and authority over the enemy in our lives and homes, in our sphere of authority.

All of us have within us that which is the enemy of God. I want to say that again because somebody reading this statement is having a hard time accepting it. All of us, born again or not, have some degree of that which is the enemy of God in us, unless you are reading this after "the change", when "in a moment in the twinkling of an eye" we are all changed (I Corinthians 15:54). The New Testament talks about that which is enmity against God. James 4:4 says that the friendship with the world is enmity against God. Do we still have any of that in us? Romans 8:7 & 8 teaches that the carnal mind and the flesh is enmity with God. Wow! Praise God I'm better here than I used to be but I still have some carnal thinking and fleshly living in me. Ephesians 2:15 & 16 tell us that Jesus abolished the enmity in His flesh. The glaring fact here is that because of our flesh we all are at enmity against God to some degree. According to the Webster Dictionary, the word enmity is a word of 13th century origin that comes from the word "enemy". What's more, James 4 says the friendship of the world is enmity with God...for that reason anyone who is a friend of the world is the "enemy" of God. This enmity against God is against our being a friend of God. Friend is a covenant word. Everything God does with, to and through man is out of covenant. Jesus abolished this enmity in His flesh. At the new birth our spirit is born again, but our flesh won't totally be renewed until the resurrection and the subsequent change (John 3:6). So, we all need some work here. What we need is the purifying and refining fire of God to penetrate into our DNA and cleanse us of generational flesh issues, as well as other issues...

Just as in the case of Israel coming out of Egypt and through the wilderness, God will reveal our enmity to us one item, or a few, at a time so as not to overwhelm us and literally dismantle our lives (Exodus 23:30; Deuteronomy 7:21-23). We are not to fear these internal enemies. God will "little by little" destroy them with His fire as we advance in Him and into His presence.

There are several areas in our lives in which we need to apply God's refining fire. First of all, we need it for our own deliverance, from generational and acquired strongholds, familiar (familial) spirits, traits and habits. God's fire can go into our very being and purge these. It is very important that, as He shows us demonic influences in our lives, we bind them, loose them from us and call down God's fire to destroy them, so they don't return later to wreak more havoc on us. It is also critical that we ask Him to take us into a deeper level of His river of fire to purge more of our own generational being, with each revelation of a stronghold in our lives. I have been amazed over the last three years as God has taught this prayer strategy to me, how He has responded to my prayer to take me deeper into His fire and do a deeper purging in my life. Wow!

We need to apply this fire to our family. With our spouse, our children, our parents and brothers and sisters, we need to take advantage of the fire of God as we pray, war and discipline. What a powerful thing to teach your children that, through Jesus as His blood-washed child, they have access to the fire of God to deal with situations and strongholds in their lives.

We need to apply God's fire to our bloodline. Regarding a huge part of the warfare we face, we are dealing with generational curses by familial (familiar) spirits in our bloodline—family spirits if I may just say it. As we bind, then loose, then call down the fire of God to destroy these in our own lives, we are also affecting the lives of our parents and grandparents who are still alive, as well as our children and grandchildren. If what we are warring against is a generational spirit and it is destroyed, then it will no longer be able to oppose any of our bloodline.

Not only do we need to apply the fire of God for purging in our lives and our family, but the region we live in. As surely as we have authority over our own bodies, so do we in the earth realm we walk. I have had a habit of walking for years. I enjoy walking and talking to the Lord. I get much revelation during these times. Several years ago we lived along the Tennessee River in North Alabama and I was growing a bit tired of the normal route I walked. I started in the opposite direction one day and I heard the Lord say to me, "Are you sure you want to walk this way?" I thought, "...well why not?" His reply to me was somewhat amazing. He said, "Are you sure you're ready for the warfare that will come if you walk that way?" I knew instantly what He was saying. "Everywhere the sole of your foot treads I've given you, but that involves warfare. Are you ready for the spirits that have to be overcome when you walk there?" I walked my old route, praising God all the way. Come to think of it, I never did walk that new way as long as we lived there. There are some battles we are not to take on. There are many battles we take on because of where we choose to go and what we choose to do. However, if we live in a region long enough God will most likely want us to encounter every regional spirit in a place to reclaim that territory for Him. The heavens are the Lord's but He has given the earth to man (Psalm 115:16). He wants us taking territory for Him. Our dominion in earth is His creative purpose for us (Psalm 8:6; Genesis 1:26-28). He does give us the land under our feet (Joshua 1:3; Romans 16:20; Genesis 3:15). The above illustration is not to discourage taking territory or put fear in anyone. It is rather to demonstrate that our very walk is seen by our Father, our Creator, as conquering. This conquering is accomplished by the fire of God according to Daniel 7:9-27.

For the fulfillment of God's purpose in us, for the Kingdom and for God's pleasure, we need to avail ourselves of this fire of God in our own lives and in our region. This may be the most compelling reason of all for us to learn to access the fire of God. Paul wrote, "...the love of Christ constrains us..."[13] The love of Christ for the Father that caused Him to set His face as a flint rock to go to Jerusalem and die to fulfill Father's purpose ought to constrain us to exercise the fire of God on His enemies.

Don't you just want relief? Don't you just want the enemy to have its due? Don't you just want payback for the enemy? Aren't you tired of the need for

---

[13] II Corinthians 5:14 (KJV)

repeated deliverance for the same issues and the same demons? I'm aware of the passage where Satan "...departed from Jesus until a more convenient season..." (Luke 4:13). I'm also aware that a season of destruction is coming for the enemy. I contend that this season is here, at least for demonic spirits that are the support structure—"the errand boys"—for ruling principalities and powers. Their day will come, too, as will the day of the Lord for the destruction of Satan and even death and hell itself.

Let us learn to avail ourselves of the fire of God. Let's avail ourselves of the fire of God for our personal deliverance, purging and restoration, and that of our family. If just a small percentage of the body of Christ would do that in a region what a release from bondage and what freedom we would begin to see. As the body of Christ uses and allows the fire of God to purge us individually, we will see our territories, cities, etc... delivered as the corporate effects of many combined individual victories takes effect.

"There is coming a day when God will judge His enemies little by little, one by one, and consume them with His fire...I believe we are at that day."

Chapter 13

Let God Increase Your Discernment

As we pursue this prayer strategy and come into an understanding of God's purpose for His fire, He takes us into a higher level of discernment. GOD MUST INCREASE OUR DISCERNMENT! Some are already experiencing this. If you are not already, you will begin to experience it as you move into this or other prayer strategies. I began to recognize that God was taking me into a new level of discernment in 2005, though it started even before that time.

Discernment is extremely important. It is an essential element of our walking out the assignment God has for us in the coming days. Jesus lived His life by discernment. It is a tool He used to move in and out among people and to avoid the pitfalls of the enemy and his strategy. It is part of what is contained in the teaching repeated four times in God's Word: "...the just shall live by faith" (Habakkuk 2:4; Romans 1:17; Galatians 3:11; Hebrews 10:38). In John 2 we see that discernment is what kept Jesus from entering covenant relationships that would derail the Father's plan and purpose for Him. John 2:24 and 25 says that Jesus did not "commit" Himself to some people because "...He knew all men... He knew what was in them." Discernment kept Jesus from distractions, ties and relationships that would have derailed or at least delayed Father's plan.

Discernment operates as a measure of faith. It is one of the gifts of the Spirit (I Corinthians 12:10; Romans 12:3 & 6). When our faith increases discernment increases, and vice versa. When we seek stronger faith, discernment increases. As we learn more of God's Word faith increases and so does discernment, and so goes growth in the grace and knowledge of Jesus. I began to ask God for the gift of "discerning of spirits" in the early 1990's...and He began to answer that prayer. I would notice myself recognizing what spirit, or spirits, were behind certain cases of sin and enslavement I was dealing with in other people, as well as in myself.

What I have come to realize is that discernment is a very practical gift from Holy Spirit. It is obvious much of the time what we are dealing with, at least on the surface. The enemy weaves a web or network of deceit, so it becomes a little more tricky to understand some of the underlying demonic influence in a given situation. But it is still very doable. The Word of God makes it easy. I'll give examples of this from my own experience and learning below. When we allow the Holy Spirit to act supernaturally on our behalf, He reveals anything we are missing in discerning the enemy we are against, at least what He wants to reveal at a given time. We can begin to walk in a new level of Christ like perception...and we must if we are going to carry out God's assignment on us in "judging" the enemy (I Corinthians 6:3). <u>We must let God take us to a new level of discernment</u>.

Jesus always knew what spirit He was dealing with when He went up against darkness or began to deliver someone. He, at times, commanded the spirit to reveal it's identity. (Mark 5:9; Luke 8:30) I don't think this is because He didn't already know. Again, John 2 says "...He knew what was in man and needed not that any man should..." tell Him. I think Jesus was letting us know the importance of identifying our enemy so that *we* could deal with it. I don't know why this is so important but I know that it is. I do know that our enemy is always darkness and light reveals darkness and once it is revealed it is done away with (Ephesians 5:13; I John 3:8). The very manifestation of Jesus, the Light of the world, meant the destruction of the devil, ultimate darkness!

Just what is "discernment?" Biblically, it is the ability to "distinguish" between spirits, to tell one from another. Some translations actually quote I Corinthians 12:10, speaking of "discerning of spirits", as "distinguishing one spirit from another." Examples are the NIV, New American Standard Version, RSV, and the English Standard Version (ESV). The Greek word translated "discerning" is "diakrisis" and it means to "distinguish, discern or judge." As this book deals with, the Word of God teaches us that we are to "judge" angels. Demons are fallen angels. We cannot carry out our assignment without the ability to distinguish-discern-judge who we are dealing with. <u>We must let God take us to a new level of discernment</u>.

Biblical examples of discernment.

At this point I want to give some examples of what I call Biblical discernment. By that I am talking about a very practical look at how to recognize and identify spiritual activity by applying Scripture. I'm talking about the discerning of spirits. In the late 1980s I began to realize that when I was dealing with sin, I was dealing with a demon. I know some won't agree with this statement but I believe that there is a demon (or the devil himself) behind every act of temptation and sin. I began to believe that years ago when God drew my attention to I John 3:8. It says, *"He that committeth sin is of the devil; for the devil sinneth from the beginning. For this purpose the Son of God was manifested, that he might destroy the works of the devil."* From this verse I realized that when I committed a sin I was taking part in a work of the devil. Since the devil is not omnipresent, it was either he or one of his demons tempting me when I was faced with temptation to sin. That realization began a new process in my walk with God. That began a new process in my understanding of the warfare Paul wrote to Timothy that we were waging (I Timothy 1:18). That opened the eyes of my mind to a new realm of victory that God has taught me to walk in and minister to others now for these 25 years. In that process I have learned that we must recognize the spirit we are dealing with in order to see it permanently defeated.

Recognizing the spirit at work in a given situation is made much easier when we simply pay attention to

Scripture. For instance, hatred in the Word of God is equivalent to murder. We see this in I John 3:15. So if a person allows hatred to reside in them they could actually be harboring a spirit of murder—at best they are entertaining a spirit of hatred. Nakedness in the Word of God is related to shame. We see this in Revelation 3:18 which talks about the "shame of our nakedness." In Genesis 2:25 Adam and Eve were said to be naked and not ashamed. Something changed after the fall that opened the door for a spirit of shame to come upon those who engage in nudity publicly. This is a part of the spiritual DNA of those involved in the porn industry...they live a life of shame, bound by a spirit of shame. Another example of Biblical discernment is with adultery and fornication. These come from lust, which is covetousness according to Romans 7:7. Covetousness is idolatry, as seen in Colossians 3:5. If we look closely at these Scriptures we see a web or a network of wickedness forming, which brings the participants into bondage to the spirits involved. So then, a person who is committing fornication or adultery is not just having to deal with a spirit of adultery or pornia but also with spirits of lust, and a covetous spirit, and a spirit (or more) of idolatry. Then, adultery is covenant-breaking, so an adulterer is also going to have to be delivered of a covenant breaking spirit. I have dealt with this spirit in the region we live in and know that this is a powerful demon, serving as an example of just what kind of strongholds of bondage people can get into by engaging in one particular sin or pattern.

We will have to come to a place of increased discernment to be able to recognize and deliver of these spirits.

<u>We must let God take us to a new level of discernment</u>.

Another example that the Lord revealed to me through a dream is that of sickness, or a spirit of infirmity. A lying spirit will always govern or rule over a spirit of infirmity that is attacking a believer in Jesus. So we must not only deliver someone who has perpetual illness of a spirit of infirmity, possibly with the same name as the sickness they bare, but we must deliver them of a lying spirit. This is founded on the fact that as believers in Jesus who have His blood applied to our lives, we have already been healed by His stripes (Isaiah 53:5; I Peter 2:24). It is a lying spirit that keeps us from the level of faith necessary to overcome this. Do not be condemned by this statement. As I write this, I am dealing with a physical illness and suffering some tremendous pain. I have warred against this lying spirit and infirmity. God is taking me, us, the body of Christ, to a new level of faith in Him, far above all principality and power...

There is one more example I want to use because I think it is so prevalent in the body of Christ, at least in America. This is the spirit of poverty and excess. I have battled with this as part of my generational heritage. I'm not sure which of these spirits would be the stronger but I do know that they work together. I questioned the Lord one day about excess. I simply asked Him to teach me about excess. He replied immediately to my spirit, almost before I finished the request, "excess is a demon that is out to destroy My people..." Wow! I knew I was battling a serious problem but had no idea how serious until I heard that. When you think about it though, how many of the problems with sin and lack of discipline we have are tied directly to doing something in excess. The Lord later taught me that poverty and excess go hand in hand...poverty tells us that there won't be enough in our future and influences us to indulge in excess, while we have plenty—sort of the "eat, drink and be merry" attitude. This is very clearly demonstrated with eating...that's actually what I was dealing with when Holy Spirit taught me this.

These are just a very few examples of how God identifies sin for us, and its source in the spirit realm. He has given us a book that is complete with the equipment we need and the armor we need to do battle, AND TO WIN! *"All scripture [is] given by inspiration of God, and [is] profitable for doctrine, for reproof, for correction, for instruction in righteousness: That the man of God may be perfect, throughly furnished unto all good works."* (II Timothy 3:16 & 17)

<u>We must let God take us to a new level of discernment</u> and He will do that as we study and meditate in His Word (II Timothy 2:15).

Jesus is positioned to reveal darkness to us.

I keep the morning watch...I have for since 2006. I have always loved mornings, but in 2006 I came into a lifestyle change and started making sure I got in bed early enough to be alert and able to meditate and pray in the morning watch. It is something I am passionate about. One morning during my watch Jesus ministered to me that the mornings were so important to us. Because Jesus is seated far above all principality and power (Ephesians 1:20 & 21) He is able to see spirits as they move, maneuver and position themselves against us in the darkness to try to oppose us in the new day.

That is why we have Scriptures like Psalm 19 which tells us that the sun in its rising is as a "bridegroom" coming out of His chamber.[14] Then in this Psalm David goes into a dissertation about the power of the Word of God in our lives over sin and evil.

Then we have verses like Psalm 63:1 and Isaiah 26:9 which say to God, "...early will I seek You..." Psalm 119:147 says: *"I rise before the dawning of the morning, And cry for help; I hope in Your word."* (NKJV™)

Psalm 5 is such an amazing chapter that teaches us about David's prayer and meditation life early in the

---

[14] Psalm 19:4 & 5 (KJV)

morning so that He could walk in victory over his enemies and live in a way pleasing to God.[15]

We even have the example of Jesus, Who would rise "a great while before day" to be alone and pray.[16]

Jesus, seated on His throne, positioned, and ready to take us to a new level of discernment, for every new season we face and every new assignment we receive from the Lord.

As our discernment increases we will be able to bind the spirits revealed to us, loose them from their victim, and call the fire of God down to deal with them. We will be able to see God's purpose fulfilled through our lives and in our sphere of operation. <u>We must let God take us to a new level of discernment.</u>

"There is coming a day when God will judge His enemies little by little, one by one, and consume them with His fire...I believe we are at that day."

---

[15] Psalm 5:3 (KJV)

[16] Mark 1:35 (KJV)

Chapter 14

All Things Tried by Fire!

Why is fire such a fearful thing?

Because it is so destructive, and so hard to control. It will totally destroy most anything. Only that which is indestructible is spared, and that means only that which is eternal is not destroyed by fire.

All things are tried by fire. This is an eternal principle we see in I Corinthians 3:13. *"Every man's work shall be made manifest: for the day shall declare it, because it shall be revealed by fire; and the fire shall try every man's work of what sort it is."*

We are to live for that which is eternal. Reading I Corinthians 3:11-15 makes it obvious that Paul is defining that which is eternal. This is related to what he wrote in II Corinthians 4 which talks about the fact that we are to live for and to look upon that which is eternal, not temporary.[17] In this chapter we see the light of God talked about. God's light is synonymous with His fire. One produces the other. Both are the environment around His throne. I Timothy 6:12 says that we are called to lay hold on eternal life. The only

---

[17] II Corinthians 4:18 (KJV)

way God can position us to live for that which is eternal is to, with His fire, purge us from the temporal. As He consumes the non eternal things from us, we become filled with the eternal. We become eternal.

God will try all things to make sure they are eternal and fire is the trying element.

Also, God's uses His Word to try us. We will look in depth at the fact that God's Word is related to fire in the next chapter, but for now let's see what God says about His Word as a trying agent. It has been tried with fire and thus has become a trying agent, bearing God's fire. This is similar to what happens to us, as we step into the river of fire around God's throne and become flaming torches for His purifying purpose. In reality, the process that purifies God's Word is probably the same process as goes on in us.

Psalm 105:19 says that when the word of the Lord came to Joseph it tried Him. If you study this verse in multiple translations and from the Hebrew text, coupled with the story of Joseph's life in Genesis, you can see that God gave Joseph prophetic dreams. He began to tell those dreams and then the trials came. He was almost killed but a merciful brother who was afraid of his father and probably had some of the fear of God intervened and Joseph was just sold into slavery. He went through one trail by fire after another until God had prepared a vessel to house the Word of God. Then God's Word which had been prophesied could be fulfilled in Joseph. Joseph was now purified and ready to be a container for the Word of God. A great example of how the Word of God that we speak tries us is found in Deuteronomy 21:5. It says, *"And the priests the sons of Levi shall come near; for them the LORD thy God hath chosen to minister unto him, and to bless in the name of the LORD; and by their word shall every controversy and every stroke be tried..."*

That is how the Word of God works in us. We hear it. By faith we receive, but faith is mixed with doubt which must be purged. Also, our beings are vessels which must be purged to contain the Word and cooperate with the Word in its fulfillment. *All resistance to the Word of God in us must be removed for it to have free course.* Paul talked about this. In I Corinthians 16:9 he wrote that there was a great and powerful door open but there were many adversaries. It is possible for us to have adversarial things in our own flesh. In II Thessalonians 3:1 Paul asked God's people to pray for him that the Word of God would have "free course". The Word of God has been tried by fire and purified completely (II Samuel 22:31; Psalm 18:30). Psalm 12:6 says *"The words of the LORD [are] pure words: [as] silver tried in a furnace of earth, purified seven times."* The Word of God will not be contained, or fulfilled, in any vessel that has not gone through that same purifying process.

As a pastor, and as a college student preparing to pastor, I used to hear preachers say that when you preach a message you need to be prepared for the devil to attack you in the area you just preached

147

about. I have had this demonstrated many times in my life. The devil had something to do with it, but he and our flesh were just instruments in God's hand to have the Word of God try us.

The Word of the Lord will try us. When the Word is spoken over us, when God gives His rhema Word to us, and especially when we receive the prophetic word of God <u>and speak it</u>, that Word will try us just as it did with Joseph.

Let us not be afraid or intimidated by this trial. Think it not strange concerning the fiery trial which is to try you (I Peter 4:12). We are already victors and this is part of the process on the road to victory.

All things are tried by fire, and God uses His Word as a means to try us.

Thank God that He does. Can you imagine binding, then loosing, then calling down the fire of God and not being prepared to withstand the heat of that same fire?

"There is coming a day when God will judge His enemies little by little, one by one, and consume them with His fire...I believe we are at that day."

Chapter 15

Fire From the Word of God

In developing our relationship with the fire of God we need to come to learn that the Word of God itself is fire. This may seem strange to the natural mind but our spirit being can certainly understand it.

This is also very really demonstrated in the natural realm. Voice audio is frequency. Fire is also frequency. Yes, I'm talking again about frequency again—waves. Audio waves are of a different frequency than fire, though some fire acts as a carrier wave for audio. That's why you can hear some fire.

When God spoke He injected sound waves into the atmosphere. God's voice is of a different frequency than our audible voice. That's why most of us have never heard the audible voice of God, but God does have voice. The Word of God is clear about that. God's voice evidently resonates at times at a frequency very near that of fire, because His Word is as a fire. Actually, I guess God's voice can resonate at whatever frequency He wants it to and needs it to in a given situation.

Jeremiah experienced this. God said to Him in Jeremiah 23:29, "...is not my Word like as a fire..." He experienced it within his own being. He said that God's Word was as a burning fire in his heart, shut up in his bones, and that it was just raging to get out and he could not keep it in. Here's the verse quoted from Jeremiah 20:9: *"Then I said, I will not make mention of him, nor speak any more in his name. But [his word] was in mine heart as a burning fire shut up in my bones, and I was weary with forbearing, and I could not [stay]."*

Then Jeremiah got to experience God's Word as fire on the giving end. God told Jeremiah in chapter 5 verse 14, *"...I will make My words in thy mouth fire, and this people wood, and it shall devour them..."* I think I need to comment on the phrase, "...and it shall devour them." (My first inclination was to leave that phrase out, because it is not my purpose here to issue warning. However, I felt I was supposed to include this phrase because God's fire does consume and destroy flesh if it is not willing to cooperate with His eternal plan and His purpose as is seen in I Corinthians 3:12; II Corinthians 4:16-18). From Jeremiah 5:14 we see that it is possible for us to live in a state where the words we speak are really God's words and they burn with fire. God is no respecter of persons. What He did with Jeremiah He'll do for us, as long as we are committed to His Kingdom purpose and what we are requiring of the Lord fits His purpose.

In addition to Jeremiah's example, another example of the Word of God being fire and devouring is in II Thessalonians 2:8. It says, *"And then shall that*

Wicked be revealed, whom the Lord shall consume with the spirit of his mouth, and shall destroy with the brightness of his coming."

Psalm 148:8 is an interesting verse that links fire to the Word of God. It refers to fire, hail, snow, vapor and stormy wind fulfilling God's Word. In other words, the elements themselves fulfill the Word of God. That means they contain the Word of God. This is like Jesus...He fulfilled the Word of God and He contained the Word of God...He was and is the Word of God. This is like us. We are told in Colossians 3:16 to let the Word of Christ dwell in us richly. Fire, then, must contain the Word of God, or at least carry it, in order to fulfill it. Wow! That's as deep into that statement as I want to go at this time. Fire fulfills the Word of God and the Word of God carries His fire!

It is with fire that God gave the law to Moses. In Exodus 19 and 20 we see that God set the stage for the giving of the 10 commandments by igniting Mount Sinai. Exodus 19:18 says, *"And Mount Sinai was altogether on a smoke, because the LORD descended upon it in fire: and <u>the smoke thereof ascended as the smoke of a furnace</u>, and the whole mount quaked greatly."* Deuteronomy 9:10 confirms the importance of this in God's mind as Moses states, *"And the LORD delivered unto me two tables of stone written with the finger of God; and on them was written according to all the words, which the LORD spake with you in the mount out of the midst of the fire in the day of the assembly."* Notice that God descended upon the mountain in fire and it was out of the midst of fire that God gave the Law. This has twofold meaning and importance: God advanced into a new place with His presence which always has a fire go before Him to burn up all His enemies, and it is from this fire of His presence that the Word of God came forth. In other words, the Word was born of fire and any offspring always bears the character of the one who gave it birth. That means that the Word of God has fire at its very foundation and DNA.

Another way of seeing this is that fire can act as a carrier for the voice of God, just like one radio frequency can serve as a carrier wave for a lower audio or video frequency. We see this example in Deuteronomy 4:10-13. This is Moses' Deuteronomy account of the above Scripture, but in the Deuteronomy account God reminds Israel that He spoke to them out of the midst of the fire. This is the record of God giving them the commandments. It is also the first time where we see it being said that God is a consuming fire.

It is very interesting that in Revelation 19:12 and 13 we see the Living Word of God with eyes of fire. Jesus, bearing the name The Word of God, is coming with eyes of fire. The Bible teaches that God watches over his Word to fulfill it and that the eyes of the Lord are in every place beholding the evil and the good. Jesus, the Living Word of God, has eyes of fire watching over all things and is the embodiment of the Word of God, to fulfill it! Whatever God has spoken over any person prophetically, Jesus is watching with eyes of fire to make sure it gets fulfilled.

Finally, in Isaiah 5:24 we find a very powerful teaching. God demonstrates to us that an attitude of despising and rejecting ("casting away") the Word of God results in the fire of God devouring the root, chaff and stubble, as well as the fruit of the lives of those who do so. This principle is demonstrated in so many examples in the Bible.

In developing our understanding and relationship with the fire of God it is critical that we develop the proper relationship with the Word of God. This starts with a foundation of respect for the Word and a recognizing that is has life-changing prophetic power for us. This attitude will be demonstrated in a commitment to frequent (I believe daily) meditation in the Word of God. The proper attitude to God's Word will be like that presented in Proverbs 8:34 which says, *"Blessed is the man that hears me, watching daily at my gates, waiting at the posts of my doors."* I know that when I'm meditating on the Word of God it is impacting and blessing my life, whether I'm aware of it at the moment or not.

As you and I develop the right relationship with the Word of God we are brought into the fire of the presence of God and His fire does its work in our lives. Let's allow the fire of God's Word to burn in us on a daily basis and as we do, we will find ourselves strengthened to engage the enemy with the fire of God.

"There is coming a day when God will judge His enemies little by little, one by one, and consume them with His fire...I believe we are at that day."

Chapter 16

Seasoning Your Environment

At the time of the writing of this chapter I was on a working vacation in a beachfront town in a coastal area with my wife. I had been aware for a few days that I was in a different spiritual environment. Then God gave me insight as to the nature of the environment in this region. I became aware the past few days that I was dealing with a covenant breaking spirit. Then, two days later, I began to have thoughts of worry about finances and the future. I knew this was related to the city I was staying in...this was evident from overhearing the conversations of people and from newspaper articles, etc...in the area. God drew me to Psalm 23 to remind myself and have me confess again that He is Yahweh Roeh and that there is no lack, but rather an abundance, as our cup overflows. However, I didn't see complete release and freedom from this until the Lord gave me a download of thought which was filled with new teaching and insight. He showed me that the area in which I was staying and working was affected by an antichrist spirit. In a moment, He revealed to me that this spirit was over the covenant breaking spirit of the region, in the fact that Jesus, the Christ, is God's ultimate covenant manifestation and this antichrist spirit fights to block the revelation of Jesus as God's covenant fulfillment and the promise of His provision so that we have more than enough. As soon as I realized this, my environment broke and I felt immediate release and relief from the deep thoughts that could have been tormenting. These kinds of thoughts can cause sudden and rash actions and decisions based in fear that take us out of God's plan and/or His timing. This spirit was a very occult spirit, as were the thoughts...they were hidden in a network of darkness and had to be uncovered.

I realized that I was living in a demonstration of how we have to season our environment to accomplish Kingdom purposes.

When we were in Barbados, November of 2009, God prompted me to include this chapter in this book. We were staying for the first time on the west side of the island and I found myself repeatedly binding, loosing, and calling down the fire of God on certain spirits. I noticed on the 2nd day on the island that the need to do this was less and less, and that the warfare against me had become less intense. God captured my thoughts and showed me that I was experiencing the victory that happens when we move into a new region and begin to enforce the fire of God on spiritual darkness in that place. The weaker spirits are consumed, and others flee because of the intensity of the heat. As lesser spirits become consumed those that were in the tier above them are now the targets as they either attack or are encountered as we advance. Sometimes there is a backlash as ruling strongholds or principalities become aware of the new opposition and send out stronger attacks. At these times we must persevere and continue the fight. We must continue to apply God's fire to these spirits that attack us and we will see battles won and ultimate victory. God's fire consumes His enemy (Psalm 97:3).

Now I was experiencing this by myself. God showed me that the more people that learn and get involved in these type prayer strategies, the more this takes over an area. It's the same principle that one can chase a 1000, two can put 10,000 to flight, and, wow, exponentially this can overwhelm the darkness in a region. What can 3, or 8 or 29 or 175 praying warriors do with this in a city. It can lead to transformation, sustained transformation if we sustain our efforts.

I believe that the more we bind, loose, and call down the fire of God, the cleaner our environment. I've lived this and seen it demonstrated in my life now for years. I believe the more people in a given area learn and practice this, the greater and more widespread the impact...the enemy becomes weaker and weaker as the demonic spirits are destroyed. We ultimately see a whole region transformed as more and more of God's people participate in this powerful and amazing prayer and warfare strategy.

I am aware that the fire of God has its affect on us and on darkness whether or not we know it or intentionally use it. I also know that God has given us the ability to use and direct His fire as a weapon on the enemy.

I once heard internationally know speaker, Lance Wallnau, say that Satan isn't getting any new demons...he can't make more of them. He stated that there are more born again believers alive on planet earth right now than all those who have gone before us put together and the kingdom of darkness is spread thinner than it's ever been trying to counter all God's people. As I listened to him speak (in June of 2008), I was already carrying this prayer strategy and knew I would be writing this book. I got very very excited to say the least to think that we are about to begin adding to this equation the actual destruction of spirits of darkness, from the smallest, until Jesus consumes the "wicked one, the man of sin", and destroys him by the brightness of His coming, and the last enemy, death, is destroyed (II Thessalonians 2:8; I Corinthians 15:26).

You and I are salt! You and I carry the fire of God! Let's season our environment!

"There is coming a day when God will judge His enemies little by little, one by one, and consume them with His fire...I believe we are at that day."

Chapter 17

Enforcing the Strategy

God has been showing me the past few months how very powerful prayer is. I keep hearing Him say to me, very subtly in my mind, "...your prayers are effective. They are having an effect." I also keep seeing results in lives that are demonstrating this. Prayer is SO POWERFUL! It is part of the weaponry that Holy Spirit inspired Paul to write about in Ephesians 6:18.

The following is a short and simple collection of prayers that enforce the prayer strategy presented in this book.

I want to say quickly that I am not one to recommend certain prayers to pray. I have long believed that the Biblical term "praying in the Holy Spirit" means praying under the direction of Holy Spirit, receiving His thoughts to guide us in formulating our prayers.

The prayers that I suggest here however, are prayers that have been crafted under the direction of Holy Spirit and have been proven very effective. Since this particular prayer strategy has been growing in me and works very successfully, having been developed in me by Holy Spirit, I want to share some of the prayers I use. They are weapons of war and victory. Hopefully they will at least trigger thought in you, and you may even find them useful as your own prayers.

The prayer I use most often.

As mentioned earlier, I find myself daily praying, "Father, in the name of Jesus I bind (name of the) spirit, and loose it from off me (or my family, staff, certain people, city, etc...) and I call the fire of God down to consume it."

Sometimes I am more detailed in this prayer, saying, "Father, in the name of Jesus I bind (name of the) spirit by His resurrection power, and loose it from off me (or my family, staff, city, etc...) by the two edged sword of the Word of God, and I call the fire of God down to consume it." Occasionally I will find myself asking for the wind of the Holy Spirit to lift this spirit up into the atmosphere before I call for it to be consumed. Now frankly, I don't know if these times represent a weak moment of faith on my part, or a need to refresh my mind as to the Biblical authority of the prayers, or if for some reason God just wants me to use a more strongly worded prayer (our words do have power), but I've learned to trust my instincts as being indicators of Holy Spirit's leading. I also at times, will ask for the angel or angels with the two edged sword to come and loose a given spirit off me, or the person I'm praying for, etc... (Added May 11, 2015 in revision: I find myself being led by the Holy Spirit for the last year or two to pray as follows, after binding then loosing a given spirit... "I loose

_____ into the second heaven and call for the fire of God to come and surround it and contain it there until You are ready to destroy it Lord.")

There are many times that I will stop short of calling down the fire of God in the above prayer, to consume a spirit or spirits. This would usually be when dealing with a principality or stronghold that I don't sense God is ready yet to destroy. That could be due to a weakness on my part...on other occasions it's just not time. As talked about earlier in this book, we are to judge nothing before its time.

I often use Jesus' Hebrew name and pray "in shem Yeshua", the name of Jesus. I believe there is amazing power in the Hebrew language. I not only use Hebrew in availing the power of Jesus' name, but in other areas of prayer and in blessing others. I would encourage you to consider this.

Binding the strong man.

I always bind the demonic strong man of any city, municipality or region I'm working in. I do this daily, or at least weekly. Sometimes I exercise that authority over a state, and sometimes a national government. God taught me the importance of this in June of 2008. I was in the Washington D.C. airport and excited to have a 3 hour layover to use to pray in our nation's capital. During that time I forgot that I had intended to intercede while I was there. When I remembered, almost at the time of my departure, I simply prayed going into the restroom a prayer like, "Lord, I pray that your government would invade and take over the government in this place." While in the restroom I slipped and re-injured my knee...the pain was excruciating. (I had a series of about 6 knee injuries between October 2007 and July 4th, 2008.) I gained my composure and limped back to find my seat to await my departing flight. While sitting there I asked the Lord what in the world had caused such a freak injury. His immediate reply was, "...you were attacked by a governmental spirit." I knew I had heard His voice, but didn't understand till later when He reminded me that I had heard Chuck Pierce say in so many words that, you cannot go into an area and exercise authority there until you first bind the strong man of that region.[18] Of course! I knew that teaching from Jesus in Matthew 12:29 and Mark 3:27. I now knew it from experience. I vowed to never forget that, if the Holy Spirit would remind me. He has...I regularly practice binding the strong man of the kingdom of darkness in any territory, county, state, nation, and city I travel. As an intercessor, I am always doing war. Actually, any believer possessing the Spirit of Christ is going to carry a warring atmosphere against the enemy. I have come to understand that this is a vital teaching of Jesus, our example and the Captain of our salvation, for anyone who is going to be a city reacher and an influencer of the spiritual climate over any region. Binding the enemy is simple...you just say it or think it, by the authority given us in Jesus and His name. When the enemy is bound his ability to deceive

---

[18] "Chuck Pierce." Glory of Zion International Ministries, Inc. Accessed June 18, 2015. http://www.gloryofzion.org/chuckpierce/.

is limited or removed (Revelation 20:1-4). This would mean that our faith to accomplish God's purpose is freed and is greater, as well as the faith of those around us.

Prayer for the fire of God as light.

Many times when I sense someone is ensnared in a web of deceit or blindness by the enemy, I will call down God's fire as light to surround them and illuminate their lives, their minds. This is also founded in the teaching of Revelation 20 when the angel binds Satan with a chain and he cannot "deceive" during the time he's bound. I use this prayer often when I sense that someone is not ready to be delivered, and maybe not even aware of the need of it. The light of God will show them their need.

Prayer for protection.

In praying for protection, for myself, my family, or others, sometimes whole cities, I will pray that God will surround a person (or people) with a wall of fire so that if the enemy approaches them, it will be scorched or consumed. I often say the prayer this way: "Father, in Jesus' name would you surround (name) with a thickened, intensified wall of fire so that any attempt of the enemy to approach or attack would consume the enemy? I am now feeling drawn to define this area of fire around my wife and me by a definite distance, a radius. I won't say how far but I often ask the Lord to thicken the wall of fire around us to a __ mile radius. This prayer is based in Zechariah where God says He will be a wall of fire around Jerusalem, and His people.[19]

Prayer for purifying fire.

I find myself daily praying that God would take me deeper into His river of fire as I approach His throne, and let His fire go deeper into my cellular DNA to do a newer and deeper work of purifying in me.

I also often pray the same prayer for neighborhoods or sections of cities. I have seen amazing subtle results in doing this. It is fun to watch people, families, communities and cities change as the fire of God enlightens those Jesus died for and consumes darkness.

Be thankful for the fire of God.

I have come to love the fire of God and not fear it, so I find myself thanking Him for His fire.

I find myself singing in worship about the fact that I'm going to bathe in His river of fire.

Again, I've never been one to recommend pre-worded prayers, although I think God does it. How many prayers do we see in Scripture, written for us to copy if we are so directed? My point above is not to

---

[19] Zechariah 2:5 (KJV)

suggest you pray these prayers as much as it is to show examples of how I've implemented the prayer strategy of the fire of God.

May Holy Spirit direct you and fill you with His words and His prayers. May you meet Him and agree with Him in prayer as He meets face to face with the Father in prayer.

> *"There is coming a day when God will judge His enemies little by little, one by one, and consume them with His fire...I believe we are at that day."*

Chapter 18

Stepping Into His River of Fire

So, there is a river of fire.

So, Jesus is the Baptizer in fire and wants to baptize us in this river.

God is inviting us to step into His river of fire, every time He beckons us to His throne.

How do we step into God's river of fire? How do we go deeper into the fire of His presence? We must look at the examples we have in God's Word for those answers.

We see pictures of God's river in both Daniel and in Revelation. In Daniel we have two pictures of entering God's fire.

The three Hebrew youths.

In Daniel 3:6-27 we see a picture of the three Hebrew children being cast into the burning fiery furnace.

Not only was it hot, but it was heated seven times hotter than ever before. And yet it did not consume them. It destroyed those who cast them into the fire, but did not hurt them. There is only one reason I can see, other than the supernatural protection of God. <u>They had reached such a state of surrender to God and become such eternal beings</u>—refined of wood, hay and stubble—that the fire couldn't hurt them.

Again, this is spoken of in I Corinthians 3:12-16 and in II Corinthians 4:16-18. In these two places we see that which can be consumed being destroyed by fire and being temporal or temporary. All else is gold, silver and precious stones, which is not destroyed by fire but is refined and made better-it is eternal. These three Hebrew youths were thrown into the fire...they didn't jump in. What caused this? They were simply obedient...they simply did the will of God. My point is that the very act of doing the will of God will lead us into the fire that tries, the fire of God. That's why all of us who are believers in Jesus have experienced some degree of the fire of God. The more our level of consecration, the more of God's fire we experience and the greater the frequency of these experiences. Sometimes we make commitments to God unaware that we have areas in our lives that cannot stand the fire we are about to encounter. This causes great upheaval in our lives and sometimes great loss. The comforting thing is that it never costs us anything eternal...fire only refines eternal things. We need to be aware of the results of our commitments, as much as is possible. That's why Jesus warns us to "count the cost" of our commitments to Him (Luke 14:25-35).

The fire of God's throne.

In Daniel chapter 7 we see another picture of the fire of God, the fire around His throne. I think it is important to read this passage so I've included Daniel 7:9-27. I've also underlined phrases that I feel are important to this discussion and used double underlines for emphasis. What we see here is a determination that God has made already that His saints, under Jesus' rule, will take the global Kingdom and rule it forever. We see this being carried out over a process of time and under a drama that goes back and forth so that if you didn't know the final result you would wonder who the winner would be. This makes me wonder if the enemy, not having a living faith in Messiah and being in darkness, actually thinks he is going to win this thing (I'm really enjoying this, sitting in a coffee shop laughing as I write.)

> V.9 *"I beheld till the thrones were cast down, and <u>the Ancient of days did sit, whose garment was white as snow, and the hair of his head like the pure wool: his throne was like the fiery flame, and his wheels as burning fire.</u> V.10 <u>A fiery stream issued and came forth from before him: thousand thousands ministered unto him, and ten thousand times ten thousand stood before him: the judgment was set, and the books were opened.</u> I beheld then because of the voice of the great words which the*

horn spake: **V.11** *I beheld even till the beast was slain, and his body destroyed, and given to the burning flame.* **V.12** *As concerning the rest of the beasts, they had their dominion taken away: yet their lives were prolonged for a season and time.* **V.13** *I saw in the night visions, and, behold, one like the Son of man came with the clouds of heaven, and came to the Ancient of days, and they brought him near before him.* **V.14** *And there was given him dominion, and glory, and a kingdom, that all people, nations, and languages, should serve him: his dominion is an everlasting dominion, which shall not pass away, and his kingdom that which shall not be destroyed.* **V.15** *I Daniel was grieved in my spirit in the midst of my body, and the visions of my head troubled me.* **V. 16** *I came near unto one of them that stood by, and asked him the truth of all this. So he told me, and made me know the interpretation of the things.* **V.17** *These great beasts, which are four, are four kings, which shall arise out of the earth.* **V.18** *But the saints of the most High shall take the kingdom, and possess the kingdom for ever, even for ever and ever.* **V.19** *Then I would know the truth of the fourth beast, which was* diverse from all the others, exceeding dreadful, whose teeth were of iron, and his nails of brass; which devoured, brake in pieces, and stamped the residue with his feet; V.20 And of the ten horns that were in his head, and of the other which came up, and before whom three fell; even of _that horn that had eyes, and a mouth that spake very great things, whose look was more stout than his fellows._ V.21 _I beheld, and the same horn made war with the saints, and prevailed against them;_ V.22 _Until the Ancient of days came, and judgment was given to the saints of the most High; and the time came that the saints possessed the kingdom._ V.23 Thus he said, The fourth beast shall be the fourth kingdom upon earth, which shall be diverse from all kingdoms, and shall devour the whole earth, and shall tread it down, and break it in pieces. V.24 And the ten horns out of this kingdom are ten kings that shall arise: and another shall rise after them; and he shall be diverse from the first, and he shall subdue three kings.

V.25 _And he shall speak great words against the most High, and shall wear out the saints of the most High, and think to change times and laws: and they shall be given into his hand until a_

time and times and the dividing of time.
V.26 *But the judgment shall sit, and they shall take away his dominion, to consume and to destroy it unto the end.* **V.27** *And the kingdom and dominion, and the greatness of the kingdom under the whole heaven, shall be given to the people of the saints of the most High, whose kingdom is an everlasting kingdom, and all dominions shall serve and obey him."*

So we see again the fire around God's throne and coming from His throne. And we see again that this fire is to consume God's enemy and the enemy of His people. It is also obvious that the fire of God is directly involved in the saints of God taking the Kingdom and setting the stage for God to rule it forever.

Enter God's fire by worship.

Now how do we enter into God's fire?

We enter God's fire when we approach His throne— this is because the fire is issuing from His throne. The environment around His throne is one of fire. As the saints are doing in Daniel 7:10 above, we simply approach His throne in worship and we are stepping into His river of fire. The fire has its effect on each of us...it tries, it purifies, it refines. Each time we approach God's throne we enter that river. Sometimes we go deeper into the fire. Sometimes Jesus, the "one like unto the Son of man" (vs. 13 above), baptizes us in that river of fire. Often when we approach, the fire of God burns deeper into us than it ever has before, purifying even more of us. We can reach a state of living in God's throne room environment so that the fire never dims or goes out. Then we become burning embers for Him and He is a wall of fire around us and His glory within the wall of fire (Zechariah 2:5). In reality, it is probably more accurate to say that when the body of Christ comes into a place where we as a whole live in this throne room state of mind, then we will be surrounded by His wall of fire. I say this because it is Jerusalem that is surrounded with the wall of fire in Zechariah 2...we are the individual stones of the New Jerusalem God is building (I Peter 1:5; Ephesians 2:20-22). Another part of this equation is that the church and Israel must come into the "one new man" God has promised for this to enter the full potential of the fire of God as a wall around us (Ephesians 2:13-22).

The same fire in Daniel 7 that strengthens us as it purifies, also has a destructive affect on God's enemy and the enemy of the saints (Daniel 7:11 & 26). So when we approach the throne of God we are in effect taking part in the destruction of the enemy. I'm reminded of Proverbs 28:4 which says, *"...they that forsake the law praise the wicked but such as keep the law contend (strive) with them."* Our very lifestyle can be one of opposition to God's enemy. Our very act of breathing is to be praise (Psalm 150:6) to God. I believe we can live in such a state of frequenting the throne of God that our very act of breathing can be fighting, warring against the enemy.

The picture in Daniel 7:11 and 26 of the saints before the throne worshipping is the exact picture John saw and painted for us in Revelation 4 and 5, that of ten thousands times ten thousands of saints worshipping before God's throne. This again emphasizes that the way we approach the throne of God is through worship, and that approach to the throne of God puts us in the river of fire that flows from His throne. In Revelation 4:5 we see another aspect of this fire. It says, *"And out of the throne proceeded lightnings and thunderings and voices: and there were seven lamps of fire burning before the throne, which are the seven Spirits of God."* So, the fire from before the throne of God is directly related to the seven fold Spirit of God. We may get a huge picture of what this means from Isaiah 11:2. It says, *"And the spirit of the LORD shall rest upon him, the spirit of wisdom and understanding, the spirit of counsel and might, the spirit of knowledge and of the fear of the LORD..."* This is speaking of Jesus according to verse 1. Jesus, Who is the Refiner's fire of the Father, the baptizer in fire, will be covered with the Spirit of the Lord, which in Isaiah 11:2 bears seven names, counting the overall name, "Spirit of the Lord". Is this the same 7 Spirits of God that burn in Revelation 4? I believe it has to be because it is upon Jesus Who is the fullness of the Godhead in a body (Colossians 2:9). This makes God's purpose for His fire very evident. His Spirit is on Jesus to give wisdom, understanding, counsel, might, knowledge and the fear of the Lord.

It's amazing to me to read the rest of Isaiah 11. After introducing us to the seven fold Spirit of God on Jesus, we see the Kingdom reign come into fullness. I believe this is a demonstration that when the body of Christ avails itself of the fire of God and makes use of it as our strategy against the enemy, we will see the Kingdom of God come into full view and power in the earth.

It is also obvious when comparing Isaiah 11:2 and Revelation 4 that the baptism of fire is related to the baptism of the Holy Spirit. This is why Matthew 3:11 and Luke 3:16 both say that Jesus will baptize us with the <u>Holy Spirit and with fire</u>. Lord, give us deeper understanding here! The Holy Spirit is inseparably related to the fire of God. It is also true, then, that the baptism of fire is necessary for the fullness of the Holy Spirit in our lives. It is necessary in order for us to walk in all the completeness and fullness of Jesus, Who was filled with the Holy Spirit. The baptism of fire is necessary for us to be possessed by God's Spirit of wisdom, understanding, counsel, might, knowledge and the fear of the Lord. I won't take the time to talk about it here, but these attributes of the Holy Spirit in Isaiah 11:2 are amazing...they are the very character of Jesus Who is the express image of the Father.

Enter God's fire through His Word.

Another clear picture the Lord gives us in the Bible is that His Word is like fire—so for us to enter into and engage the fire of God, it is imperative that we have the right relationship to the Word of God. Chapter 15 of this book is given to this. You may want to read that chapter again as you meditate on your relationship with the Word of God. I speak of having a "relationship" with the Word of God almost as if it's a person who has feelings. In fact, I believe God does the same thing concerning His Word. In Proverbs 8:36 He says concerning the wisdom of the Word of God, *"But he that sins against me wrongs his own soul: all they that hate me love death."* This verse can be translated literally to say that whoever ignores, neglects or rejects God's wisdom is "mistreating" his own soul. I had my introduction to the term "mistreat" as a child growing up when my brother would tell Mom or Dad that I was mistreating Him. This is a term used to describe relationship. In our relationship with the Word of God, when we mistreat the Word we are doing harm to our very own soul. When we pursue and nurture a relationship with the Word of God we are bringing the purifying, refining, holy fire of God into our lives. We are strengthening our lives and developing an eternal culture about our life. We need to review our life as it relates to the Word of God and ask Him to strengthen that area of our lives. His Word, brought into our lives as we meditate on it, brings the fire of God into our lives. *"As you and I develop the right relationship with the Word of God we are brought into the fire of the presence of God and His fire does its work in our lives."*

Enter God's fire by the baptism of Holy Spirit.

There is a very clear link in the Word of God between the baptism of the Holy Spirit and the baptism of fire. In Matthew 3:11 and Luke 3:16 we are told that Jesus would baptize us with fire and with the Holy Spirit. The two are linked.

In II Thessalonians 2:8 God tells us that when "the wicked one" is revealed Jesus will "consume (him) with the spirit of His mouth."

These are passages that link fire, or fire terms, with the Spirit of God.

When we desire to go deeper into the fire of God and have it go deeper into us, we must have a greater immersion in Holy Spirit. If you desire more of God's fire in your life seek a new baptism in Holy Spirit. Ask God to fill you with His Holy Spirit to a new level. He promised us that if we'd ask He would do that. Luke 11:13 says, *"If ye then, being evil, know how to give good gifts unto your children: how much more shall your heavenly Father give the Holy Spirit to them that ask him?"* Do not over think this. God says that if we, being evil...ask Him to fill us with Holy Spirit, He will. Do not let sin in your life keep you from asking Him to fill you to a new level with His Spirit. He will send His fire to purify you in new ways and then fill you with Holy Spirit to new levels. Jesus will baptize you in the Holy Spirit as He baptizes you in His fire.

Ask the Father to take you deeper?

When we approach the throne of God we are, *in the spirit,* coming to His throne, to the mercy seat, and to the Ark of the Covenant. This is born out specifically in Hebrews 8, 9 and 10. Hebrews 9:23 and 24 even us the words "pattern" (sign or symbol) and "figure" (type) to describe the fact that the ornaments in the tabernacle design God gave Moses represent the environment of God's presence in Heaven. Hebrews 9:24 puts it so plainly when it says, *"For Christ is not entered into the holy places made with hands, which are the figures of the true; but into heaven itself, now to appear <u>in the presence of God</u> for us..."* Jesus has entered the true tabernacle and appeared before the true Ark of the Covenant, God's throne, where we find the cherubim angels overshadowing the mercy seat, <u>in the presence of God</u>. As we have detailed in this book, the presence of God is an environment of fire, the same fire that consumes the sacrifice on the alter at the Ark of the Covenant. It is to this setting that Father urges us to come in Hebrews 4:16. *"Let us therefore come boldly unto the throne of grace, that we may obtain mercy, and find grace to help in time of need."* How often have we run to God's throne for mercy and grace to help us in a time of need, not knowing that we were running to His river of fire—even possessing a fear of the fire of God while we ran toward it.

Would you now take some time to talk with the Father about going deeper into His fire? Would you ask Him to prepare you to go deeper into His river of fire? Would you ask Him to increase your discernment to make you more aware of His fire and your need of it in your life? Do not fear His fire. It will not harm you if you are surrendered to His Kingdom and covenant purpose...it will refine you and purify you so that you become an eternal vessel of His fire to take it to those who need it and to pour it on the enemy so that it is consumed. A fire goes before God and consumes His enemy before His face. As you and I appear more and more in the presence of the Lord His fire will consume the enmity that is in our flesh and we will become greater carriers of the presence of the Lord and will be walking fiery furnaces burning with His presence and consuming the enemy in our paths.

I want to encourage you to continue to step into His fire. I'll remind you of the following illustration from Saturday, February 13, 2010:

> *This past Saturday the Lord gave me a very real demonstration of the fact that there is a fire that is invisible and yet is still burning. I went outside and it was an overcast and cold morning. All that was missing was the snow. I felt so instantly drawn to build a fire in my chiminea. I hadn't planned on it...it was a sudden urge. I usually don't respond to those but it was Shabbat so why not. I thought I'd build a fire and sit and meditate and talk to the Lord a bit. As I began to light the fire and would touch the lighted match to the newspaper the fire would go out, instantly, as if someone or thing*

was blowing it out. This happened three times, with three matches. I was about to get frustrated as I was lighting the fourth match and I noticed smoke coming from under the newspaper. Within a few seconds the paper ignited and was in full flame. Now I've started several hundred fires in my lifetime but I've never noticed anything like this. I've never had the kindling blow out the fire before. The Lord grabbed my attention and let me know that He had orchestrated this whole ordeal, drawing me to start a fire, to demonstrate to me that even though my eyes cannot see it, there is a fire that burns and is effective that will accomplish His purpose.

There is a fire that is invisible and yet completely effective for God's purposes.

Would you step into His river of fire?

"There is coming a day when God will judge His enemies little by little, one by one, and consume them with His fire...I believe we are at that day."

Conclusion

Develop a Relentless Pursuit of Your Enemies!

There is coming a day when God will judge His enemies little by little, one by one, and consume them with His fire...I believe that day has arrived and the Lord is preparing us to play our part in that process.

We have discussed how God draws us to His throne of grace so that we step into His river of fire and, when we do, we become the fire of God. You have by now made a decision...you will either pursue the fire of God in and for your life or you will back off to avoid it, at least for a season. You will either intensify your access to the fire of God and use it to war against your spiritual enemies, or you will try to avoid it for now.

I often remember hearing Chuck Pierce, of Glory of Zion International, say something like this: "...we're not supposed to take on every demon...just the ones that get in our way."[20]

---

[20] "Chuck Pierce." Glory of Zion International Ministries, Inc. Accessed June 18, 2015. http://www.gloryofzion.org/chuckpierce/.

Amen! I agree. We cannot be hindered by God's enemy, our enemy, from fulfilling the purpose God has laid upon us. It is His Kingdom purpose. It is the greatest thing there is. God has given us the authority to possess the Kingdom. That means we dispossess the enemy who may now hold it. Jesus has purchased this authority for us and granted us the power of His name to do it. His Kingdom WILL endure and conquer and last forever (Daniel 7:14 & 18).

As I was wrapping up work on this book and had finished, I thought, with all but the edits, the Lord illuminated to me in my Bible reading one morning Psalm 18:37. It says, *"I have pursued my enemies and overtaken them: Neither did I turn again till they were consumed."* I knew I had to add that to this manuscript.

God wants us to develop a relentless attitude in pursuing our enemies. They are His enemies. This attitude is part of the mind of Christ that we are to have, because Jesus and the Father are intent on the destruction of Satan and all his demons...every enemy that has opposed the reign of Christ.

In Psalm 18 we see God as our rock, fortress and deliverer. We see Him as the one Who saves us from our strong enemies which were too strong for us, and who had gone before us to set a trap for us. Then comes verse 37. It is clear that God's desire for us is not only to deliver us from our enemy, but then fill us with His life and power, and surround us with His fire, so that we are employed to destroy His enemy, and our enemy. Again, Psalm 18:37 says, *"I have pursued my enemies and overtaken them: Neither did I turn again till they were consumed."*

Speaking about God, Psalm 21:8 & 9 state, *"...Thine hand shall find out all thine enemies: thy right hand shall find out those that hate thee. Thou shalt make them as a fiery oven in the time of thine anger: the LORD shall swallow them up in his wrath, and the fire shall devour them."*

When we take on the mind of Christ, Who always heard and did what was in the mind of God the Father, we will partner with Him in this attitude. We may not spend our time looking for the enemy but when, in the course of doing Kingdom business we meet the enemy, we will seek the heart of God as to how to see the enemy devoured in the fire of God.

Will you ask the Father now to bring you into the place where you have a relentless pursuit of your enemy, until it is destroyed?

"There is coming a day when God will judge His enemies little by little, one by one, and consume them with His fire...I believe we are at that day."

About the Author

Michael David Riggs was born in 1957, in Florence, Alabama, USA.

His father was a pastor and his mother a teacher. They taught him the Word of God from the earliest age. They taught him the importance of the Word of God and prayer as part of a daily lifestyle. They imparted to him a love for the Word of God. At the age of 3 Michael trusted Jesus as his savior, an experience which is still very vivid in his memory.

After high school he attended technical school at what is now Northwest Shoals Community College in North Alabama. There he studied electronics technology and did work toward an associates degree in applied science, graduating in 1977.

At the age of 19 Michael surrendered his life in service to Christ. He attended Free Will Baptist Bible College in Nashville, Tennessee, then attended and graduated from Hyles Anderson College, Crown Point, Indiana, in 1983, with a BA in Pastoral Theology. While in college, Michael began doing interim associate pastoral work. After graduating from college he began serving as pastor and worked in the marketplace while doing so.

In 1993 he began a career in radio and then in 1996 he and his wife started a business which is called Perfect Praise, Inc. They have developed a preschool piano program, training babies and young children to worship Jesus through music.

Michael continues to use his pastoral and teaching gifts in the marketplace and to advance the Kingdom of God in cities and nations.

Michael and Denie Riggs have 5 children, 10 grandchildren, and live in Huntsville, Alabama, USA.

They are aligned with Chuck Pierce and Glory of Zion, commissioned as both a Business of Zion and a House of Zion.

Bibliography

"Hebrew Lexicon :: H784 (KJV)." *Blue Letter Bible.* Accessed 10 Jun, 2015. http://www.blueletterbible.org/lang/lexicon/lexicon.cfm?Strongs=H784&t=KJV.

[2] "Greek Lexicon :: G1210 (KJV)." *Blue Letter Bible.* Accessed 10 Jun, 2015. http://www.blueletterbible.org/lang/lexicon/lexicon.cfm?Strongs=G1210&t=KJV

[3] "Greek Lexicon :: G3089 (KJV)." *Blue Letter Bible.* Accessed 10 Jun, 2015. http://www.blueletterbible.org/lang/lexicon/lexicon.cfm?Strongs=G3089&t=KJV

[4] II Peter 3:8 (KJV)

[5] Luke 19:13 (KJV)

[6] "Greek Lexicon :: G4231 (KJV)." *Blue Letter Bible.* Accessed 10 Jun, 2015. http://www.blueletterbible.org/lang/lexicon/lexicon.cfm?Strongs=G4231&t=KJV

[7] "Occupy." Merriam-Webster.com. Accessed June 10, 2015. http://www.merriam-webster.com/dictionary/occupy.

[8] Isaiah 66:16 (KJV)

[9] Daniel 7:26 (NASB)

[10] Ruth 2-3 (KJV)

[11] Romans 12:1 (KJV)

[12] Romans 8:28-31 (KJV)

[13] II Corinthians 5:14 (KJV)

[14] Psalm 19:4 & 5 (KJV)

[15] Psalm 5:3 (KJV)

[16] Mark 1:35 (KJV)

[17] II Corinthians 4:18 (KJV)

[18] "Chuck Pierce." *Glory of Zion International Ministries, Inc.* Accessed June 18, 2015. http://www.gloryofzion.org/chuckpierce/.

[19] Zechariah 2:5 (KJV)

www.ingramcontent.com/pod-product-compliance
Lightning Source LLC
Chambersburg PA
CBHW051726040426
42447CB00008B/1000